# The
# Addams
# Chronicles

# The
# ADDAMS
## Chronicles

Everything
You Ever
Wanted
To Know
About The
Addams Family

# STEPHEN COX

**Harper**Perennial

*A Division of HarperCollinsPublishers*

Grateful acknowledgment is made for permission to reprint artwork on the following pages: page 3, © 1946, 1974 The New Yorker Magazine, Inc.; page 4, © 1962, 1990 The New Yorker Magazine, Inc.; page 7, © 1940, 1968 The New Yorker Magazine, Inc.; page 31, © 1964 TV Guide and News America Corporation.

FIRST EDITION

*Designed by Cassandra J. Pappas*

---

Library of Congress Cataloging-in-Publication Data

Cox, Stephen, 1966–
The Addams chronicles : everything you ever wanted to know about the Addams family / by Stephen Cox. — 1st ed.
  p.   cm.
ISBN 0-06-096897-4 (paper)
1. Addams family (Television program)   2. Addams family (Motion picture)   I. Title.
PN1992.7.C68   1991
791.45'72—dc20                                                                           91-55315

---

91  92  93  94  95  DT/CW  10  9  8  7  6  5  4  3  2

*Cheers!*
*To the One whom I admire most:*
*The Father, Son, and Holy Ghost.*

*Courtesy of Howard Frank Archives*

 Contents

# Acknowledgments

*Merci beaucoup!*
*("Tish, that's French!")*

 As Gomez Addams always welcomed strangers into his creepy home, the same unconditional hospitality was displayed when I approached the ensemble who created this classic. For you, I do what Gomez might do . . .

Present a cigar? Nahhh.

Clenches of money? God, no.

I *can,* however, offer a zestful, half-cocked Gomez grin and a personal, hearty expression of gratitude to:

Tee Addams, John Astin, Jefry Abraham, Howard Anderson, Ken Beck, Jami Bernard, Carol Brady, Herbert Browar, Tom Brown, Kevin Burns, Bruce Button, Ramona Christophel, Mark Collins, Gerald and Blanche Cox, Archie Dalzell, Bruce Davies, Al Dusing, Jeffrey Forrester, John Franklin, Leslie Coogan Franklin, Rick Gibson, Linda Gray, Christopher Hart, Tom Hansen, Luther Heggs, Carol Henning, Paul and Ruth Henning, Frank Inn, Raul Julia, Dave Kahn, Sammy Keith, Vicki Lemp-McDonald, David Levy, John Lofflin, Lisa Loring, Tony Magro, Sandy Mailliard, Patty Maloney, Kevin Marhanka, Vic Mizzy, John Nicholaides, Sandy Oliveri, Salvador Pequeño, Nat Perrin, Vito Scotti, Felix Silla, Al Simon, Howard Smith, Fredrick Tucker, and Marge Weatherwax.

A special thank-you to those individuals and organizations contributing illustrations: ABC-TV; Mrs. Tee Addams; Cato Johnson Advertising; Howard Frank Archives/Personality Photos, Inc.; Hanna-

Barbera Productions, Inc.; Milton T. Moore Photos (P.O. Box 140280, Dallas, TX 75214); the Museum of Broadcasting in New York City; *The New Yorker;* Orion Motion Pictures and Television Syndication, Sunsoft Corporation; *TV Guide*/Triangle Publications, Inc.; and Universal Studios/MCA.

A warm round of applause for the special assistance from Jennifer Hull, Tod Machin, Bob Morris, and my editor, Craig D. Nelson, who enjoyed the show when he was young and continues to appreciate its humor. And thank you to Kim Lewis, Patrick Dillon, Cassandra Pappas, and John Fontana for all their production editorial, copyediting, and design expertise.

Grateful acknowledgment is made to the following for permission to reprint special materials: John Callaway (PBS); *Starlog* magazine; *TV Guide*/Triangle Publications, Inc.; and Vic Mizzy for the "Addams Family" lyrics.

# Foreword

 Without asking for it, Charles Addams and I shared a mutual destiny punctuated in our separate, private lives by legions of unknown young people who, upon learning of our identities, would snap their fingers and chant a bouncy tune neither of us wrote called "The Addams Family Theme."

As a child, I was fascinated by Charles Addams's cartoons. I would ponder them for stretches of time, not really understanding my curiosity, as they gradually enhanced my own obsession with trying to understand the nature of life itself.

In college we sometimes bought double copies of the Addams books, from one of them carefully razoring selected cartoons for framing.

When I heard that they wanted to make a TV series based on the cartoons, it seemed almost sacrilegious to me, and the first meeting rather confirmed my fears. I was told the show would be built around the "adventures" of the butler, whom I was to play, presumably with lifts and lots of padding and makeup.

But later that day the show's executive producer, David Levy, called me to a cocktail tête-à-tête at the Polo Lounge of the Beverly Hills Hotel. With Addamsish eyes and a slightly wicked grin he told me he wanted me to play the father, assuring me he held a similar respect for the cartoons, to which he promised we would remain faithful.

But how could that be accomplished? For example, the drawing of the family on the roof about to pour molten whatever-it-is on the carolers below, is one exquisite moment. We can savor the frozen scene, but what happens next? In film we must carry forward. Do we show the "oil" falling and the carolers writhing in pain below? Of course not.

Fester waves ahead a car following him on a treacherous mountain bend right into the face of an oncoming truck. Do we show the crash?

Morticia stands at the neighbor's door: "May I borrow a cup of cyanide?" An extraordinary moment, as she stands there in her black silk gown. But what happens next?

What was the essence of the cartoons? And how could they be translated to film?

Addams himself, at the request of David Levy, had provided a written character sketch of each family member and, for the first time, had given them names. Describing my character as a "rather jolly fellow," he gave us a choice: Gomez or Repelli. We chose Gomez. "Pubert" as the name for my preadolescent son was rejected by the network and he became "Pugsley." But the descriptions were all too brief. The key to the puzzle lay in the cartoons themselves.

Studying them more and more, I decided that these enigmatic works of art with captions were, in a sense, an attack upon the cliché through the device of implied violence. But the violence was never actually *committed*. There was no pain, nor agony, nor real unhappiness. There was, in fact, a celebration of the unconventional in a world of conformity.

Beyond all this, however, the cartoons awoke in me an appreciation of the commonplace event: of the moment-to-moment wonder in daily life itself. To me, the Addams cartoons had nothing to do with horror —which is why I feel the scores of imitators haven't come close.

I concluded that Charles Addams's cartoons were, finally a celebration of life, and in the character of Gomez I did my best to capture that spirit. In fact, understanding the tendencies of episodic television and the "grinding out" of "entertainment" that it necessitates, I determined to develop for Gomez a personality so strong that it would be able to override not only a poor script, but even a perversely out-of-character one as well. That is, no matter *what* they wrote for me to say, I would be able to perform it *in character*.

Fortunately, this was rarely necessary, obviated by the omnipresence of Mr. Levy and the inspired writing of Nat Perrin, who joined us in time to extend our presentation film a few minutes to compose the first episode. Auditions and screen tests produced Jackie Coogan, Ted Cassidy, Blossom Rock, Ken Weatherwax, and six-year-old Lisa Loring, each one unique and perfect. But still no Morticia until, finally, the flash of insight to offer the part to Carolyn Jones!

So we became a "different" family, strange, weird, unconventional, generally eschewing the clichéd. We would look askance, perhaps, at the Boy Scouts, but ah, the wonder of a spider and its web! We were mutually supportive in our "madness," and Gomez and Morticia were the first married couple on television who seemed actually to have a sex life. I had proposed that their romance be unceasing and in the grand manner, that the slightest look or a key word send Gomez into raptures.

Psychologists and psychiatrists wrote in a plethora of articles, that, while possessing a bizarre exterior, we were internally quite sound as individuals and as a family. They said we were, in fact, the *healthiest* family on the air. Perhaps this helps explain the show's sustained popularity after so many years, and how that collective destiny has brought us all to Steve Cox's amazing encyclopedia of Addams Family history. I hope you enjoy browsing through it as much as I did, stopping here and there, flipping backward and forward from reference to reference, jogging memory and yearning, almost as I contentedly mull over the baseball encyclopedia on a quiet, balmy summer evening.

Charles Addams's lovely wife, Tee Addams, told me, shortly after his passing away in 1988, of a cartoon in a Boston newspaper. The Addams Family was standing, weeping, around a headstone titled "Charles Addams," while in the corner of the panel, Charlie, with a grin on his face, was digging his way out.

I'll be looking for you, Charlie, and thank you for helping *me* look for the mystical, awesome, inscrutable, wondrous detail of life, and for the limitless joy within myself.

JOHN ASTIN
*Los Angeles, California*
*June 21, 1991*

# Tour de Force

*It would be a waste of time to attain total sanity. I don't even have an image of sanity. It's a mistake to have one. This madness isn't confined to actors and show business. Plumbing contractors and insurance salesmen, for instance, are faking sanity. The whole world is a collective maniac acting out a charade or pretending to an image of sanity.*

— *JOHN ASTIN*, **Actors About Acting, Loving, Living, Life**

 I must be insane to write this book. That thought entered my mind on more than one occasion during the preparation of these pages. After all, screening the shows for thirty-two hours while analyzing an antagonizing and altogether absurd—albeit amusing—array of Addams Family paraphernalia can be hazardous to your psyche. But wonderful.

It's a sophisticated show, this "Addams Family" (although I hope that labeling it so is not detrimental to its future appeal to the masses). Regardless of that, an audience was there from the moment the show aired in 1964 and stayed loyal throughout its run of but two worthy years. Not many realize it, but this short-lived production claims an ensemble of classic, legendary, and unique talents pooled to produce a show that mirrored the diverse creativity of its members. From the actors to the production team, here are an elite few who remain exemplary in my estimation.

Think of it: Jackie Coogan was the movies' first child star. Producer

Nat Perrin, who for many years wrote for the inimitable Marx Brothers, boasts a career filled with exemplary films and TV shows. Listen to the masterpieces of Vic Mizzy, scribe of the show's theme song and music, and you recognize a truly inimitable Hollywood sound: no one else can recreate his music, because he's got "the secret," he says—and it's true.

Credit must be given to cartoon genius Charles Addams, the devilish developer of these kooky characters. His artwork remains in a class by itself.

Think of legendary Ruby Levitt, multiple Academy Award nominee for set decoration, whose sets for *The Sound of Music* and *Chinatown* as well as—yes—"The Addams Family" remain masterworks. Or how about executive producer David Levy, who invented the show and imbedded his creative fingerprints in the program? Levy, former vice-president in charge of programming at NBC, was the man responsible for putting motion pictures on television.

*Signed publicity photo of the cast (Courtesy of Tony Magro)*

These talented folks, among others, are collectively responsible for producing one of the most off-the-wall, impulsively dynamic, and ingenious programs ever aired on the explosive medium known as television. Now, for the first time, you will experience a peek into the assemblage of this unusual, innovative, and sometimes daring situation comedy and into its subsequent cult following. You will meet others who claim they understand the show and "Addamantly" adore it. And I hope you will be entertained along the way. I was . . . but in the most ironic of means.

Wherever Addams led, it seemed Evil followed. Evil in a most mysterious and harmless facet, let's say. Visiting the monstrous front of a spooky Victorian house recently constructed for the new Addams Family feature film was eerie enough. A fierce, steady wind shrilled toward the San Fernando Valley as it kicked up smoke and dust on the Burbank bluff where the lone Addams mansion stood. The house overlooked the city—which you couldn't discern through the smog and clouds. The house's shutters flapped, and the effect was graveyard as I approached the made-for-movies mansion: I felt a chill shock when I actually heard the "Addams Family" theme song in the air. A guard was whistling it to himself as he pulled his hood over his head because it looked like rain. Amidst several years of successive drought conditions in Los Angeles, for photographing the outside of this creepy mansion I happened to choose a day when a sudden downpour nearly killed my opportunity.

Later that very day, I visited the hilltop hideaway of music maestro Vic Mizzy, who composed the show's snappy theme. Who would imagine I'd witness this mad music scientist pounding the organ keys in a dark room with the console's intense light shining into his eyes while shadows flickered across the room? The darkness pressed down upon us as Mizzy, his back to me, played his unforgettable, bizarre organ melody from *The Ghost and Mr. Chicken* and themes from such other shows as *The Spirit Is Willing, The Night Walker,* and of course "The Addams Family." Visions of the Phantom of the Opera kept haunting me. The house vibrated as he created the illusion of a twenty-piece orchestra. I dreamed of secretly peering over his shoulder to spy blood-stains on the ivories (". . . and they used Bon Ami!"). Spooky cartoonist Charles Addams, on whose characters the show is based, would have savored these ironies—among secret others that haunted me.

At Christmas time, 1991, the most powerful medium—motion pictures—finally welcomes the Addamses, and moviegoers will experience the Family in a full-length feature film. Too bad it's not Halloween.

I introduce you to the family Addams.

STEPHEN COX
*St. Louis, Missouri*
*July 30, 1991*

# Charles Addams:
# Master of the Macabre

*I'm not particularly a fan of his TV show. By the*
*very nature of television, it got bogged down with*
*gags and low-comedy plots. However, I rather en-*
*joyed Charles Addams cartoons much better.*
*They're wonderful. I never met him, but I heard he*
*was an amusing little fellow.*

*—VINCENT PRICE*

 Conjure these images: A nurse congratulates a brand-new father in the hospital waiting room; holding up the newborn, she says, "It's a baby!" Or how about the housewife who relaxes while gossiping on the telephone after shooting her husband, who lies inert at her feet—"And what's new with you?" she asks. Or maybe the cannibal mother consulting the tribal medicine man about her small boy. "I'm worried about him," she confides. "He won't eat anybody."

One summary of a Charles Addams book contends, "Creeping in and out of these pages are some of the most despicable characters. How in the world they ever became lovable—every last parent-murdering . . . potion-brewing one of them—is a mystery known only to Charles Addams and countless thousands of his fans."

Lord of his own genre, cartoonist Charles Addams has been described as an elixir "brewed out of the essence of Edgar Allan Poe, Aubrey Beardsley, Dorothy Parker and Alfred Hitchcock" (Sarah Booth Conroy in the *Washington Post*). He spawned an entire generation of

*Master of the Macabre:*
*Charles Addams in 1953*
*(Worldwide Photos, Inc.)*

off-the-wall dark-humor cartoonists, including *Playboy* magazine's
Gahan Wilson and Gary Larson of "The Far Side."

His name has become part of the American language. "An Addams
house" describes a gloomy old Victorian mansion inhabited by a variety
of horrors, goons with surplus arms, and tiny people, among question-
able creatures. Addams found humor in horror and expressed it with
the pure, contagious excitement of a rascally boy who has just planted
a spider in his sister's bed. He allowed us to look at the flip side of
every day, at the shadows that creep at night. He was regarded as the
funniest spokesman for all the repressed violence that lurks in society.
His work made light of dark humor and thrived on incongruous juxta-
positions. He was wicked without harm, both affectionate and sardonic.
For more than five decades, this real Grisly Addams exhibited to the
world a veritable museum of the macabre through his cartoons, which
gained speed with audiences when they were first published in the
classy magazine *The New Yorker.*

Writer Brad Darrach explains that we smirk at a deliciously gruesome Addams cartoon because

we all have a fiend or two tied up in the emotional basement. Probably we laugh because we see our own carefully hidden ghouls in Addams' monsters and feel a glorious relief when our terrible secrets abruptly erupt into the light—and turn out not to be so terrible at all. That is the heart of Addams' appeal, the reason millions treasure his cartoons as personal epiphanies. In an age of anxiety, he caught us unawares, helped us befriend our worst fears and offered us the absolution of innocent laughter.

Believe it or not, this gentle man, who physically resembled a cross between Walter Matthau and Lyndon B. Johnson, was the first to promote death as a leisurely concept. "I think it's alright to die," Addams once said. "It's something we all face, so we might as well have a laugh out of it if possible." He was the first to illustrate human departure as hip. Today, with coffee-table pictorials on death (*Sleeping Beauty* and

*Scoring in Heaven*) and a successful hearse-driven Hollywood Graveline Tour that escorts victims on a detailed death watch of celebrities' final steps, the topic has become an outward intrigue rather than a hideaway. What is usually tucked inside the forbidden zone is now open for discussion. Books reprint morgue photos with little regret (a morbidly sharp final photograph of Marilyn Monroe on the morgue slab was featured in one recent biography). Celebrity death certificates sell by the thousands in Tinseltown, while grave-site-seeing at Forest Lawn has become a staple of the tourist trade in California (maps are sold that advertise, "Get within six feet of your favorites"). Celebrity casket snapshots appear on the covers of supermarket tabloids, and tastes in the topic range from mild to garish. Death has become "fashionable," if you will, in the 1990s.

Although Addams cartoons are devilishly funny, his ingredients left most of the macabre to the imagination. While he definitely pioneered perversities, with a dash of humor and a pinch of realism, his work never bordered on a Freddy Krueger nightmare.

Recognizable at a glance, his artwork had exquisite range—from

*"Suddenly, I have a dreadful urge to be merry."*

the darkest black to the purest white—and the impact of an Ansel Adams photograph. It was executed with insidious skill and a strategic lure. Addams often painted in the unorthodox method of top-to-bottom; and his images, whether painted or sketched, were painstakingly detailed with shadows, tones, and mood, and weirdly animated in his unique style. His composition was "solid," say art critics. The glorious architecture that Addams featured were buildings that actually could be built, while, naturally, his favorite landscape was a graveyard.

What bizarre species of person would bring to life such characters as his, so unsavory, so bizarre? Most people familiar with the Addams wit cling to the belief that he's probably demented or demoniac. "According to one report, which enjoys wide credence in Manhattan's artistic circles," writes John Kobler in his humor book *Afternoon in the Attic,* "Addams is subject to cyclic lunacy, the approach of a seizure being signalized by some surpassingly eldritch overtone in his work." Herbert Browar, associate producer of the television show bearing Addams's name, says, "There was a story about Addams that he used to have these nervous breakdowns periodically. And they always knew at *The New Yorker* when he was gonna have one because he'd come in with a particularly macabre cartoon."

Recalls Browar: "Evidently, one time he came in with a cartoon that was [set] in an alleyway with a door open next to a brick wall with a light over it. In the doorway was a nurse holding a baby in a blanket, and facing her was this sinister person. The caption was 'Don't wrap it, I'll eat it on the way home.' Now, you have to be pretty off-the-wall to think up something like that." Legend says that this cartoon was repeatedly submitted to the *New Yorker* editors by Addams, and repeatedly rejected. Some say he never actually composed this cartoon, but his reputation for savoring a gruesome joke or story fed such lore. Addams, it's been said, took enormous delight in the legend—and to promote his whimsical image as a lunatic, he periodically answered fan mail on the letterhead of an imaginary institution, the Gotham Rest Home for Mental Defectives. Admittedly, Addams did enjoy frequenting mental asylums to chat with the inmates. "They have a refreshing conversational approach," he said.

Despite his fascination for the sinister, the twisted, and the bizarre, Addams was a gentle man with a hearty laugh that's well remembered around the offices of *The New Yorker*. When he laughed, he looked toothless, but indeed his chompers were in place.

Contrary to the canard, Addams was brought into this world by the same fashion as ordinary mortals. Born on January 7, 1912, in Westfield, New Jersey, he weighed in at eight pounds. His baby book, preserved for posterity by proud parents, documented his remarkable good nature and his initial utterances of "Ma-ma." "I like to think of it as a coincidence," he told reporter Virginia Sheward in 1970, "that Mother's entries in my baby book came to a screeching halt the day she gave me my first box of crayons."

Charles Samuel Addams was an only child. His father, Charles Huey Addams, the wholesale manager of a piano company, died when the young Charles was but twelve. His mother, the former Grace M. Spear, never quite understood her son's doodlings of cannibals, ghouls, and monsters, he said. As a young boy, he indulged in books by Edgar Allan Poe and Arthur Conan Doyle, which may have laid the ground for his interests. "I was an all-American boy," he states. No traumas warped his childhood. He had fun frightening people when he was young, "but never badly." His grandmother was the recipient of one of his pranks, he recalled: "We had a dumb-waiter in our house in New Jersey, and I'd get inside on the ground floor and then very quietly I'd haul myself up to grandmother's floor and I'd knock on the door. When she came to open the door, I'd jump out and scare the wits out of her."

Although he was interested in medicine, art tugged with stronger magnetism. He drew cartoons for the Westfield High School newspaper, *The Weather Vane*; later, he attended Colgate University in Hamilton, New York, transferred to the University of Pennsylvania and wound up at Manhattan's Grand Central School of Art in pursuit of his interests. While still a novice at the Central School, he blindly submitted a cartoon he'd sketched to *The New Yorker,* with little hope of its being accepted. His expectations were so dim, he didn't follow up on the submission for months. When he finally did, he learned it was scheduled to run in the February 6, 1932, issue.

While tackling more cartoons and submitting them to periodicals, he also worked in the layout department of MacFadden Publications, which, to his delight, marketed a mystery and crime magazine. He

inserted lettering and retouched photographs and diagrams of the spot where a dead body had been found. He lamented the job of touching up the bodies so they wouldn't seem too ghastly, "because a lot of those corpses were kind of interesting the way they were." By the later 1930s, his cartoons were appearing regularly in *The New Yorker* and other publications; he quit his day job and remained a freelance artist the rest of his life, contributing to *Collier's, Life,* and *Holiday* magazines among many others.

His first real hit—and possibly still his most famous cartoon—appeared in *The New Yorker*'s January 13, 1940, issue. It depicted a lady skier who passes a tree, leaving tracks around both sides of the tree. Reportedly, years later the cartoon was adopted by a Nebraska asylum as a test for mental-age levels and incipient insanity, which tickled Addams's funnybone; yet the cartoon's mass appeal continually baffled the illustrator. "I was always surprised it had such a worldwide response," Addams said in 1981. "If you take it too seriously, you're in bad shape."

His pop masterpiece and longest-running characters were the Addams Family, who first saw the dark of night "around 1937," he recalls, in a cartoon of yet unnamed Morticia, Lurch, and a visiting vacuum salesman (Lurch started out with a beard). Later Addams refined the first two characters and added the husband, the kids, and Uncle Fester.

In an interview with PBS correspondent John Callaway in 1981, he explained the origins of this famous brood.

"Morticia was sort of an ideal for me. It was a kind of good looks that I appreciated at that time, and still do, really," admitted Addams. "Eyes slightly up-centered, and dank, snakelike hair. She's the strength of the whole family. She's not patterned after anyone in particular, although I've often thought there was a little Gloria Swanson in her.

"Uncle Fester . . . is, in effect, me, because I think he looks like me—or that's the way I feel that I look, plus a little more hair. . . . As far as the grandmother is concerned, it could have been my Grandma Spear in the early morning, just before breakfast. Gomez, well, I don't think he looks like anyone I ever saw. But 'Gomez' was the name of an old family friend. And Lurch, well, he's, you know, the stumbly butler who never speaks. . . . And the little boy . . . was originally named Pubert, but his name was changed to Pugsley, because I think when we made some dolls, the people who were pushing the dolls felt that 'Pubert' was a dirty word. I don't know why."

When the Family became a successful television show in the 1960s, the characters were withdrawn from *The New Yorker* due to "the snobbishness of editor William Shawn," one reporter speculated. Addams assumed the magazine felt the characters might be "too thinly spread." For the TV rights to his characters, Addams was paid $1,000 a week, plus percentages on the merchandising of the characters. Although he enjoyed the television production, his newfound exposure, and the wide response to the program, he later openly regretted the deal he had made with David Levy and Filmways Productions. "It was an unfortunate contract. I don't get anything from [the show] anymore. I didn't have a theatrical agent at the time, so it was not too foresighted."

What rights to the television series and the characters Addams did maintain were hastily signed over to his second wife in a divorce settlement—another move he wound up regretting. It's been said that Addams adored his Morticia character so much that he married her. "I married someone that certainly bore resemblance. In fact, I married two of them," he told Callaway. "I privately knew it was a type of look that I liked, but I didn't marry them just for their looks. . . . But, after all, Morticia's not a bad-looking girl."

His charm, wit, and fame made Addams a popular escort between his marriages; he was seen about New York with celebrities such as Joan Fontaine, Jackie Onassis, and Greta Garbo. Married and divorced twice (to model Barbara Day, and later to attorney Barbara Barb), he wed his third wife on June 1, 1980, in a pet cemetery. The former Marilyn Matthews Miller, known as "Tee," wore black for the nuptials, while he sported a dark suit and sunglasses à la the Blues Brothers (he had just been treated for a detached retina).

Whether his marriages ever inspired his cartoons, which were frequently doused with spouse killing, no one knows for sure. His ideas came from a variety of sources, but 95 percent of them were his own. "Things occur to you on the street, or during conversation," Addams said. "Of course people send in ideas which you can sometimes use. I remember there was a minister in North Carolina who used to send in ideas regularly. But they were so sinister that I was horror struck . . . and they were unprintable. He kept them coming for a year or so. . . .

"I dream ideas. The only trouble is, you wake up and it's useless or in bad taste, or both. And I had one idea come to me while I had a hangover." (It's a Family drawing of a delivery man carrying the children—locked in portable pet kennels—home from camp.)

According to his friend the novelist John O'Hara, Addams was easygoing, with "a decent contempt for the opinions of mankind. He speaks with a New Jersey twang, plus a drawl of his own, and but for the grace of God, which gave him his enormous talent, his sense of humor, and his impatience with banality, he might have become a successful politician."

Addams had two personal phobias that threatened his sense of security—claustrophobia and fear of snakes—and he focused cartoons around both of them. Slithering boa constrictors "obsess him so thoroughly that he will spend half a day in a snake house, rooted in horrid fascination," commented writer John Kobler. Late one night, Addams accidentally trapped himself in an elevator at the *New Yorker* offices by shoving the levers the wrong way. With no elevator man on duty, he panicked, sweat pouring down his face, before he jammed the machinery into operation again. Seemingly average on the outside, this genius of wit maintained he was "all-American," albeit he had some quirks. He admitted that cemeteries were hard to resist investigation.

"There's a romance about old tombstones," he said.

Unusual sights, events, and objects—of which he collected many—always piqued Addams's interest. His house truly was a museum, filled with sinister bric-a-brac, ancient instruments of torture, and an expensive collection of sixteenth-century crossbows, which he practiced shooting. "I have this fantasy," he said, smiling. "A robber breaks into my apartment and just as he comes through the door, I get him—right through the neck. *Always* through the neck."

Addams was thrilled to the bone when he savored two fascinations at once—crossbows and snakes—by spearing the second with the first. But crossbows composed just one area of his personal decor, which defied any classification except "Addamsesque." He scoured junk and antique shops for years, amassing a Manhattan penthouse filled with ancient Maximilian armor (circa 1505), a collection of brass lizards, skulls, and an early human thighbone weapon—a Christmas gift from Tee. In the center of one room was a "drying-out table," otherwise known as an embalming table, from 1863, which he converted to a coffee table. His desk boasted an unusual paperweight—a fragment of a tombstone, inscribed "Phoebe 1780." His treasure trove of collectibles included a rosette of human hair framed with the explanatory inscription: "Abe Lincoln's hair his father's and his mother's his sister's hair please do not destroy this was made by Nancy Green in the year 1888."

One of his favorite items, which he referred to as "Stephen," sat under glass in his living room: a rare demountable twelve-inch model of the male anatomy used by medical students of the nineteenth century, its innards ready for dismantling, the intestines resembling a walnut.

His passion for automobiles—fast automobiles—led to his collecting them through the years: a little blue Bugatti from 1929, an Aston Martin, several Mercedes-Benzes. He enjoyed speeding his little autos around Manhattan and zipping into the countryside. He rarely raced professionally, except, as his friends say, the races he organized—Addams versus all the other cars on the road.

On September 29, 1988, Addams hopped in his Audi and blasted off to Connecticut to visit friends. He hastily returned to the city and parked outside of his apartment house—and slumped onto the steering

*Charles Addams was an aficionado of medieval paraphernalia, vintage original crossbows, and archaic instruments of torture. An old embalming slab served as a coffee table in his Manhattan suite. (Personality Photos, Inc.)*

wheel when his heart gave out. Ironically, this artistic genius who made a career of having fun with death was dealt his demise while having fun.

Charles Addams requested no unusual epitaph or bizarre locale for his final rest. He *did* request that in lieu of a somber funeral, a party be given, which it was. At the New York Public Library, a festive tribute to the cartoonist was thrown, complete with a Dixieland jazz band. Many celebrities, friends, and cohorts attended and paid tribute to the man—including John Astin, a star of the TV series, who delivered a few lines for the eulogy.

When asked in the early 1980s how he'd like to be remembered, Addams said, "As a good cartoonist, is all I ask."

There remains no argument over that.

*Charles Addams at a summer Sunday charity function, 1987 (Courtesy of Joan Baron)*

## *Books Illustrated by Charles Addams*

*Addams and Evil* (Simon & Schuster, 1940)

*Drawn and Quartered* (Foreword by Boris Karloff; Random House, 1942)

*Afternoon in the Attic* by John Kobler; pictures by Addams (Dodd, Mead & Company, 1943)

*Monster Rally* (Foreword by John O'Hara; Simon & Schuster, 1950)

*Homebodies* (Simon & Schuster, 1954)

*Night Crawlers* (Simon & Schuster, 1957)

*Dear Dead Days* (A book of drawings, photos, and deadly tales; G. P. Putnam's Sons, Inc., 1959; paperback edition, Berkeley Medallion series, 1966)

*Black Maria* (Simon & Schuster, 1960)

*The Groaning Board* (Simon & Schuster, 1964)

*Chas. Addams' Mother Goose* (Windmill Books, Inc., distributed by Harper & Row, 1967)

*My Crowd* (Simon & Schuster, 1970)

*Favorite Haunts* (Simon & Schuster, 1976)

*Creature Comforts* (Simon & Schuster, 1981)

How fitting that Addams churned out *thirteen* books of his works!

# A Father Appraises
# His Progeny

*Author's note: This article, written for* TV Guide, *was run in an October 1965 issue featuring John Astin and Carolyn Jones dancing the tango with their cartoon alter egos on the cover. Grateful acknowledgment to* TV Guide/News America Publications, Inc., *and Mrs. Tee Addams for allowing me to reprint the text.*

Before the Addams Family appeared on television . . . it had been a subject for speculation among magazine readers and, notably, the late *New Yorker* critic Wolcott Gibbs, who wrote in 1947:

> The thoughtful reader . . . will wonder about the inhabi-
> tants of that crumbling Gothic pile known, at least to me, as
> the 'Old Charles Addams Place.' What dark and shameful com-
> pulsion brought the proprietors together—the haggard ruined
> beauty and the ignoble half-breed? What unspeakable rites
> united them, if wed they are at all? We know their little girl
> has six toes on her left foot, that her younger brother likes to
> mix his childish poison brews, and that their only playmates

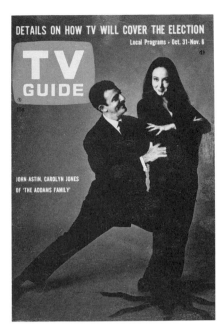

Reprinted with permission from **TV Guide**® magazine, © 1964 and 1965 by
News America Publications, Inc., Radnor, PA

are bats and spiders and probably The Thing that has no face
but wails and drags his chains at night. And we know still less
about the shambling giant who ministers their dreadful needs,
except that he is apparently dumb and almost certainly a homi-
cidal maniac.

Mr. Gibbs concluded that on the whole he thought the glimpses
from the printed page were enough, and indeed in 1947 he was undoubt-
edly right. Now, on television, in what some of us like to think is the
Decline and Fall of the American Family, we find ourselves faced by a
group who certainly put up a united front against conformity, and the
result is a peculiar form of self-identification.

In rereading the characterizations I did for the show, I find the
special flavor of each has been preserved.

Morticia, for example, was to be beautiful and aristocratic, the real
head of the family and the critical and moving force behind it. Incisive
and subtle, she is given to low-keyed rhapsodies about her garden of
deadly nightshade, henbane and dwarf's hair. She indulges the mischie-

vous activities of the children but feels that Uncle Fester must be held in check.

Gomez is a crafty schemer but a jolly type in his own way. Sentimental and often puckish, he is full of enthusiasm, and a firm believer in the survival of the fittest. Wednesday, child of woe, is wan and delicate, with her mother's black hair and dead-white complexion. Quiet and sensitive, she loves picnics at the underground caverns. Pugsley is an energetic, pop-eyed boy and a dedicated troublemaker.

As for Lurch, this towering butler has been a morose presence about the house forever. He is not a very good butler but a faithful one. The children are his favorites and he seems to guard them against good influences at all costs.

Granny is foolishly good-natured and easily led, and some family troubles are due to her weak character.

Uncle Fester is incorrigible and, except for the good nature of the family and the ignorance of the police, might be under lock and key. His complexion, like Morticia's, is dead white. The eyes are piglike and deeply imbedded and circled unhealthily in black. Without teeth and absolutely hairless, he has a peppery manner and a high-pitched voice.

The casting has been superb, and Carolyn Jones and John Astin, as heads of the household, are beyond my reproach.

# A Walk on the Wild Side

It all happened so unceremoniously. David Levy, a former NBC executive, was walking down Fifth Avenue in New York City one cold, winter morning. As he stopped to peek at a bookstore window display, a newly released collection of Charles Addams cartoons caught his eye, and he went in to investigate. Levy picked up a copy of *Homebodies* and thumbed through the crisp pages. He didn't chuckle. His mind was too busy charging with an electric idea: this might be great for TV. Levy quickly pulled out his wallet and purchased the book. Knowing that on television this family could not quite match the macabre flavor of the book, he nonetheless was sure the idea would work with a bizarre instead of malevolent set of Addamses.

As he told writer Michael Shore, he called the offices of *The New Yorker* and set up an appointment to meet the cartoonist. "We spent two hours over drinks at the Oak Room in the Plaza Hotel," Levy remembers. "Addams was tall, young looking for his age, with a twinkle in his eye. He was modest, laid-back, spoke laconically, and had a very dry wit.

"I remembered a famous quote of his," Levy says. "He was emerging from a big screening of Liz Taylor's *Cleopatra* with actress Joan Fontaine on his arm, and he was asked if he enjoyed the movie. He said 'Yes.' What part? 'I liked the asp.'

"I had all this in mind when I met him, but for two hours we spoke of nothing but novelist John O'Hara. Seems Addams and O'Hara had been drinking buddies since Prohibition. I knew O'Hara from trying to

17

do some of his stories on TV. I gathered that Addams had been approached about TV shows before but had been diffident, and the O'Hara connection is what endeared me to him.

"Addams said, 'Let's meet again tomorrow to discuss this. At my place.' So next day I went to his place—a little fifth-floor walk-up atop a small Manhattan apartment building. It was a pretty Addamsy place, with suits of armor in the living room, a huge collection of antique crossbows, and so on. I told him that since he'd never named the characters in the cartoons, I would need names and character sketches. A few days later, we met again and he had it all down on paper. Except for the husband's name—he had 'Gomez,' but he also had 'Repelli,' for 'repellent.'

"And that was it. Addams never had any further input or feedback after those first meetings."

Amid a flurry of activity that ultimately led to casting, David Levy sat at endless meetings with network executives, producers, writers, and the like. Although Addams had reserved for himself the right to veto casting decisions and make alterations in the series, he usually complied with all of Levy's choices. Levy took his show to Filmways Productions, which had already had a string of successes in its stable, airing hits such as "Mr. Ed" and "The Beverly Hillbillies," with more popular shows on the way. Al Simon, vice-president of Filmways, met with Levy to discuss the show and its direction. Levy, responsible for placing such shows as "Dr. Kildare" and "Bonanza" on television, knew exactly what he wanted. He envisioned this family, molded the idea, and became the root of the project, with power in almost all matters surrounding production.

The show differed greatly from the cartoons. Its vision was not as macabre as Addams's; the Family's television house was to be positively wacky, unlike Addams's cartoon mansion with its dark, somber Victorian style. In fact, the television show was almost animated in its intent, while the *New Yorker* strips were low-key; in essence, the show would be a cartoon of a cartoon.

It was Filmways that approached John Astin and called him to attend a special brainstorming session. As Astin recalls, it was late January in Los Angeles. Also present in Al Simon's office were Simon, Marty Ransohoff, the head of Filmways (sitting at Simon's desk), and John

Calley—all of whom Astin knew—and one person whom he didn't know.

"As I understood it the purpose of the meeting was to interest me in doing the show," says Astin. "There was a guy sitting in a straight-back chair in the center of the room. He was introduced as the executive producer of the show. His name was David Levy. I said, 'I'm sorry, but I don't know you. What have you done?' David didn't bat an eye. He explained his credentials.

"Marty said basically, 'We want to build the series around the butler,' " Astin recalls. " 'We want you to play the butler. We'll give you a nonexclusive contract.' I couldn't believe this deal they were offering me!"

As an actor, Astin was willing to try anything. He had just come from co-starring in the canceled sitcom "I'm Dickens . . . He's Fenster" and had a wife and kids at home. He needed to work, to act, and, of course, to pay the bills and support a family. But Lurch, he thought. Astin was familiar with the Addams cartoons and had been a fan of his wild sense of humor for years.

"Frankly, I walked out of the meeting thinking, 'Well, this will never happen,' " Astin says. "Marty drove by and yelled something like 'Non-exclusive contract!,' waving at me from his car. . . . I got home and the phone rang. It was David Levy. He said, 'Could you meet me for cocktails at the Beverly Hills Hotel Polo Lounge this evening?' "

"Sure," Astin agreed.

"We sat down. Levy told me he saw the series differently. He was really interested in my playing the father in the series. . . . The idea was interesting, and we began to discuss the possibilities with this character," Astin says.

Carolyn Jones was offered the role of Morticia after a string of unsuccessful auditions that turned up no one who suited Levy. Jones seemed hesitant at first, but finally became intrigued by the offer. Alice Pearce, the original chinless Gladys Kravitz on "Bewitched," auditioned for the role of Grandmama but was rejected because she was too young. Blossom Rock got the role. Famous female impersonator T. C. Jones auditioned for Uncle Fester, but he didn't fit the mold, either.

As Jackie Coogan's daughter Leslie Coogan Franklin describes it, her father rarely went for auditions in his career, but Fester was a part

*Coogan and Fester: Originally, the makeup artists blacked out Fester's teeth, but later they decided to forgo the routine. (Personality Photos, Inc.)*

that for some reason he desperately wanted. "Jack went in and wasn't offered the part," she says of his initial meeting with producers. "He went home, got in a costume, shaved his whole head, did his makeup the way he pictured it would be, because he was an Addams fan from the cartoons. He went in with the high-pitched voice, the makeup, and costume all on his own. The producers sent everyone else home. It was a bit humiliating to him, I think, that he had to prove himself, but he obviously wanted the role."

This was late February 1964. By March, a filmed "presentation" (condensed version of a complete pilot) had to be cast, shot, and ready to show at the National Association of Broadcasters convention in Chicago. It was hastily shot at MGM Studios on a mildly redressed set from the film *The Unsinkable Molly Brown,* which had just wrapped, and featured the regular cast and guest star Allyn Joslyn as a truant officer who visits the home. The train-wreck scene reused in many subsequent episodes was filmed for the presentation, as was the shot of Gomez filing the gate in front of the house, used in the opening of

*Filing the gate while filming the pilot presentation. The real house behind Gomez was never used again in the series. (Personality Photos, Inc.)*

each episode. Behind Gomez was a filmed backdrop of a real house, an old mansion that stood, coincidentally, on Adams Boulevard in Los Angeles.

After a wildly successful screening of the fifteen-minute film at the NAB convention, the show was purchased by ABC-TV network, and the cast and crew moved to permanent ground at General Service Studios. A set was built on Stage 8 that would become their asylum-away-from-home for the next two years.

David Levy recalled to Australia's *TV Times* in 1965:

I'll never forget the day we showed Charles Addams the presentation film. He had to approve it before we could continue work.

It was in New York. I had taken the film there and we met in the projection room of NBC studios at Rockefeller Center. Addams had three lawyers with him, I was by myself.

Right away, when the film started, I knew I had the law-

*Producer and writer Nat Perrin, tanned and fit at age eighty-six in 1991 (Photograph by Stephen Cox)*

yers on my side, since they almost fell off their chairs laughing. Addams just sat there, stonefaced. When the show was over, one of the attorneys turned to Charlie and said: "Levy has made the Addams family more real than you have, Charles." Addams smiled. I knew then we were on the right track. He liked it.

Fighting deadlines, the whole ensemble involved with the Addams show worked long hours to get episodes into the can. Writer extraordinaire Nat Perrin, a Hollywood mainstay with a long history of writing for the Marx Brothers, was enlisted as the show's producer. Unbeknownst to audiences, Perrin actually wrote much of the dialogue as well. This was an extremely difficult show to put on paper; it took careful hands to prepare lines for these oddball characters that preserved the flavor of the Addams cartoons while accommodating the alterations that Levy had made in adapting them for TV. Perrin took the scripts submitted by writers, punched them up, and rounded the edges, making each of them an appropriate "Addams script," he said.

His rapport with the writers was very good, because he enhanced their material and they knew it. But he never claimed any credit.

"Writers have a lot of limitations," says Perrin. "They script and rewrite within a certain amount of time and to a point, [then] you had to take over yourself. I participated in the scripts. And I think that's a very important function. I would never hire a producer for a weekly television show who couldn't write and have the ultimate responsibility for the script. I may have screwed up scripts, but you do the job as best you can."

Many times Perrin was called to the set to salvage a situation. "They'd say, 'The scene isn't working,' and I'd give them a new scene in what they considered miracle time very often," he says. John Astin readily recalls several funny "instant" telephone conversations written by Perrin for Gomez to fill in a few minutes of time. Anyone peeking into Perrin's office at any moment might find him flapping his arms wildly, racing around the room, spouting lines and material while his

*The stars study the script with writers Ed Ring, Carol Henning, and Mitch Persons. (Courtesy of Carol Henning)*

stenographer put them on paper. He worked quickly, which is what the "Addams" set required.

There was one instance, however, when Perrin regretted not placing his name on a script. "I felt it was totally unfair," he says of the incident. "I wrote one hundred percent of the script, outside of, say, the background. It happened to be the script of a very close friend of David Levy's. This guy needed money. I liked the guy, and he was a good writer, but not in this area. David said to me, 'Oh, let him have the credit.'

"I said, 'David, that's worth ultimately five thousand bucks! He didn't do the script! I don't steal credits from writers, but why shouldn't I have it?'

"Levy said, 'Oh, it's beneath you.' I said, 'Oh, well, okay,' and let it go.

"I rarely have regrets," Perrin admits. "But occasionally—and especially when residuals come around."

Carol Henning, daughter of producer Paul Henning, worked at Film- ways one summer in the publicity department, "when women were hired as secretaries and actresses only." She and an associate assem- bled a clever idea about Cousin Itt's problem of shedding hair and approached associate producer Herb Browar about working the treat- ment into a script. Cowritten with Mitch Persons, an eighteen-year-old mailroom boy at the studio, and Ed Ring, Henning's boss, "Cousin Itt's Problem" remains one of the funniest "Addams" episodes. In all, the series employed more than twenty writers and story contributors, most of whom came and went quickly each season.

Just as the show attracted a diverse mass of sponsors (everything from Dow Chemical to Bristol-Myers, Clairol to Pepsi-Cola, Union Car- bide to the Florida Citrus Commission), nearly every episode featured a new director. Veteran director Sidney Lanfield came closest to being considered a steady on the set. The late Lanfield was from the old school of directing, says John Astin. "He would be maybe less than considerate to some of the supporting players," says Astin. "That was the subject of some discussion between the two of us. But I loved the way he enjoyed the show and laughed. Sidney would set up a great shot and let us work within the shot. He didn't stop for an overabundance of close-ups. . . . All of us wanted him there to direct."

*Character actor Vito Scotti, who played Sam Picasso among other roles, immensely enjoyed working on "The Addams Family." (Photograph by Stephen Cox)*

Character actor Vito Scotti, a little Italian who's appeared in almost every sitcom ever made, beamed on "The Addams Family" three times and supported the stars in the TV reunion video in 1977. On "Gilligan's Island"—as Boris Balinkoff, the mad scientist, and a near-blind Japanese soldier ("You fogga my grasses")—Scotti made a record four visits to the uncharted desert isle, more than any other guest star.

Scotti had an initial aversion to Lanfield. "I had the great displeasure of working with Sidney Lanfield on another show, 'The Deputy,' before 'Addams,' " he says. "Lanfield always looked for a guy to pick on in front of the crew and in front of the cast. He picked on me one day. I'm a very quiet person. And he started in—'All right, you don't know the difference from your left foot and camera right!' He just went on and on. He tried to make me look like an idiot. Finally, after one scene, I beckoned him quietly. Without anybody listening, I said, 'You pick on me one more time, I'll throw you on your fuckin' ass right on the center of this stage. You believe me I can do this?' He said, 'All right, Mr. Scotti. Let's continue,' and the scene went on. Things were okay after that.

"Then I get a call for 'The Addams Family,' " says Scotti. "I get to the set and who the hell faces me—Sidney Lanfield! I thought, 'Oh shit.' All of a sudden, 'Mr. Scotti! Welcome to the set! A chair for Mr. Scotti! Coffee, Mr. Scotti?' He was a sweetheart."

Scotti (whose roles on "The Addams Family" included the seedy artist Sam Picasso, who sells out for mere money) enjoyed his association with the show. And since they invited him to return, the producers must have enjoyed it too.

"You couldn't wait to work on that set," Scotti says of the "Addams" atmosphere. "Everybody was fantastic. Carolyn Jones—everybody used to call her 'Mother.' She was wonderful. When I went to her funeral, she was so beautiful still, even though she had suffered with an illness so."

Scotti retains affection for all of the shows he appeared on in the 1960s. "Those old shows," he says. "You look at them now and think, 'They really *were* wonderful.' They were fantasy. Now, everything is so real to life, and not funny. It's happening all around you, so what's the entertainment? Television is no fun anymore."

*Herbert Browar, associate producer of "The Addams Family" and "Mr. Ed," holding a favorite souvenir, one of Mr. Ed's horseshoes. (Steve Cox)*

As "The Addams Family" progressed, the cast shot one, sometimes two, episodes per week, which is pushing it by today's standards. The show sat relatively comfortably in the ratings seats but never became a continuously overwhelming hit. "It had tremendous muscle," recalls John Astin. Alas, it was canceled by ABC in 1966 after just two seasons and 64 episodes. This move stunned everyone on the show, who expected to return for a third season. Levy was livid. At the beginning of the show's run he'd been quoted in *The New York Times* as quite "confident" of a five-season tenure. Levy never forgave the decision makers.

"The only explanation I ever got from anybody at ABC," says Herb Browar, "was 'demographics.' At that time, this system was just sprouting, and every other word was 'Demographics show this' and 'Demographics don't show this.' It was demographics time. They felt the ratings had dropped, and if they kept it on the air, [they] would continue to drop."

Over time, a strong, cultivated audience maintained a love for the program during its run in syndication. A powerful following in Australia, possibly stronger than in America, keeps the show on the air and a

*John Astin in 1977, when he was starring in "Operation Petticoat" on ABC (Courtesy of John Astin)*

favorite down under. Though it's not widely seen in the United States anymore, an interest in the show and its characters remains.

Says Australian Bruce Davies, a hardcore Addams buff, "The main reason for its success in Australia, I believe, is it was shown on the most popular TV network at the time, TCN-9. Its charm and very subtle wit grabbed audiences down here. 'The Munsters' was too American for us down here. We had a different lifestyle."

In 1988, during a revival of the show down under, "The Addams Family" returned to television opposite "Wheel of Fortune," which was the winner in that timeslot—until the Addamses reappeared. Capturing the timeslot, "The Addams Family" was welcomed to the city of Melbourne with parties, a new wave of cult merchandise, and the opening of a Morticia Boutique Dress Shop. A punk band calling themselves The

*Reprinted courtesy of Cato Johnson Advertising and Sunsoft, Inc.*

Fester Brothers even toured with mild success. One TV network aired an exclusive live interview, via satellite hookup, with cast members John Astin, Lisa Loring, and Ken Weatherwax, telecast from Astin's home in Los Angeles.

The only surviving star from the show, John Astin, is still pestered by fans for autographs. Astin entered a new dimension on April 1, 1989, when, once again dressed as the pin-striped spook, he hosted a segment of the Nickelodeon cable network's Nick at Nite "Sitcom Zone." During "two hours of time-warped humor, bizarre coincidences, and odd behavior amongst TV Land's favorite characters," Astin introduced episodes of popular reruns—including his ex-wife's "The Patty Duke Show."

Commercials haven't forgotten the Addamses either. There was the clever Tostitos corn chips spot that inserted footage of Fester chewing and such. And one of the most ingenious ad campaigns to appear recently debuted around Christmas 1989, produced by the Cato Johnson agency for Sunsoft Corporation, a licensee of Nintendo. Fester's Quest Nintendo game cartridges were pushed in a wonderful commercial that resurrected Thing to act as huckster. The popular spots, produced by Tom Hansen in Chicago and filmed in black and white, exposed Thing busily playing Nintendo, holding the controller in front of a TV screen. Naturally, the theme song was rerecorded and utilized to trigger an instant audio reaction from viewers. "The kids loved the game, and it was a great seller," says Hansen. "But there are thousands of adults who remember the TV show who also secretly play Nintendo in their homes. So it was a nice combination."

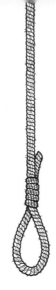

# "Their House Is a Museum...."

*TV Guide* said of the Addams abode:

> When Morticia Addams embarked upon decorating her home, she boldly set the mood with a burst of dramatic and unexpected furniture arrangements, a palette of pungent colors calculated to put to rest pastel prettiness, a trunkful of inherited goodies, a precious cache of *objets d'art,* all topped off with an inspired blending of the traditional and the bizarre, to metamorphose potentially inert space into a veritable triumph of eclecticism.

Whew! And that about says it.

Truly one of the most bizarre sets in television sitcomdom, the Addams home, located on 0001 Cemetery Lane—next to a graveyard, of course—was the pride of the city. This was a veritable Disneyland with laugh tracks. The family delighted in their palace of play, and anyone was welcome to visit.

One critic wrote, "The house was a cross between a carnival funhouse and a chamber of horrors." Indeed, the home boasted a gallery of paintings, plants, and paraphernalia that one might use to decorate a penthouse today. The decor was described by some as ahead of its time, but others maintained the homestead belonged in Bellevue. It was homey, and uniquely crafted. The butler's bellpull dangling from the ceiling was delightfully shaped as a noose (although Lurch often entered

the room under premonition as a thundering bong shook the premises). There were family heirlooms, medieval lamps, and wild tabletop center-pieces. Each room contained a box, sometimes gold-studded and handsome, for Thing to make his entrance.

A giant two-headed turtle trophy in the center of the family room was a familiar presence to visitors. Lurch's harpsichord—a wonderfully detailed gold-and-white shell, not a real instrument—rested on ornately designed Oriental rugs, while Morticia's wicker chair remained a mainstay at the center of the action. An elephant hoof temptingly filled with popcorn waited invitingly beside the staunch, steerhorn-girded armchair. Also in the main room was an Eskimo totem pole ("Cousin Nanook's family"). The walls were adorned with a variety of odd spectacles, such as a painting of a giraffe in a tuxedo ("He used to be a friend of my daddy's," Wednesday explains), and above the mantel was Pierre, the prized moose head with one whimsically bent antler. Guard-

*Jackie Coogan clowns on the set with the giant bear, one of the largest killed at the time. (Courtesy of Howard Frank Archives)*

ing the Addams premises was Bruno, a bearskin rug that growled when stepped on.

Most noticeable as you gazed at the room's layout was the hastate head of a swordfish mounted on the wall. What's so unusual about a mounted fish? This one protruded directly out of the wall, with a man's leg sticking out of the fish's mouth as though being swallowed. Gomez was proud of that beaut. As the story goes: "Cousin Ferook was a skin diver. He dived out of a rowboat in an attempt to spear a rare species of eel. At the same moment, a big fish swept up from the depths, also after the eel. They were on a collision course . . . and the rest is taxidermy."

This was not the only preserved creature in the house. Besides the king cobra candle holders on the mantel, there remained one suspicious gigantic centerpiece: the Bear.

As Herb Browar explains, a furry beast was on the set from the beginning. "For the original pilot shot at MGM, the prop department used a large brown bear, but wouldn't sell it to us for the show. I thought, 'How the hell am I gonna get one of these bears?' I called a museum, and through a whole bunch of detective work I got hold of a guy who was a multimillionaire hunter who hunted polar bears. He had a bear in storage in Seattle—it was the largest bear ever shot in Alaska up until that time. The only reason we got that bear was the hunter had recently shot a slightly bigger bear, so this one was superfluous. That's all he cared about—having the biggest bear."

For the first season, the oyster-colored bear was dyed dark brown. During the second season, the brown bear was dyed powder-white, because a darker animal blended with the background, producers said. C'mon now—*nothing* blended in that house. Every piece was as stark and striking as the lights in a carnival funhouse.

If particular props were not accessible for this unusual set, they were built to the specifications of the talented set decorator, Ruby Levitt. For another popular haunt in the Addams house, the playroom, Levitt provided the setting of an old torture chamber, complete with an iron maiden, a rack, a medieval flail, a bed-of-nails chaise longue, and stocks marked "His" and "Hers." Oh, yes—for the children there was a rocking unicorn.

Levitt brought not only class and sophistication to the Addams home but a multitude of talent and experience. "Ruby was a marvelous woman," says Herb Browar, "and a great tennis player. She had only one fault—she had expensive tastes."

Ruby Rebecca Levitt came to Hollywood in 1942 after graduating from the Pratt Art Institute in New York and some professional experience as a store window dresser. Her first job in entertainment was at Universal Studios, where she remained for several years, working on such features as the Ma and Pa Kettle films, the Francis the talking mule series, Abbott and Costello's *Lost in a Harem* (for MGM), *Bonzo Goes to College, Three on a Match, You Gotta Stay Happy, Letter from an Unknown Woman,* and many more.

Levitt was a dedicated, discriminating decorator who shopped endlessly to capture the distinctive guise she envisioned. Her life was devoted to her talent, and co-workers describe her as possessing an unequaled sense of elegance and taste. Although her own home was a small, refined, modestly decorated house in Los Angeles, she was privately hired to decorate the homes of Doris Day, Janet Leigh, and Kim Novak, among other celebrities. During her career, she amassed eight Academy Award nominations for set decoration, for classics such as *Smashup: The Story of a Woman, Pillow Talk, The Sound of Music, The Andromeda Strain,* and *Chinatown.*

After her sixties stints at General Service Studios decorating sets for "The Addams Family" and "Mr. Ed," she continued working freelance in the movies into the seventies, on films such as *Tell Them Willie Boy Is Here, New York, New York, Murder by Death,* and the Barbra Streisand *A Star Is Born.*

Tragically unable to speak or see due to a massive stroke, Levitt, now in her mid-eighties, resides in the Motion Picture Country Home and Hospital.

So the question remains—whatever happened to the fantastic, fun items that once adorned the Addams domicile? Did Jackie Coogan have the bed of nails shipped home? Did John Astin sneak out of the studio with a flail and a suit of armor? Was Morticia's peacock wicker chair privately prominent in the Jones mansion for years? At most busy studios, the set is struck the minute a show is canceled. For this show, however, the dismantlers were largely the studio executives, employees, visitors, and others who had looted the "Addams" soundstage almost as soon as the cancellation was announced. Those lucky enough to swipe fragments of the exceptional set have probably passed them down among families and collectors. Ted Cassidy stashed one of Thing's boxes, which was bequeathed to Jackie Coogan's son when Cassidy died. Jackie Coogan left the studio with his one and only Fester costume and stored it in mothballs. After Coogan's death, his widow sold it to a collector. Original props and pieces are tucked away in attics across the country, no doubt. TV fans and collectors would *kill* for them—and the Addams Family, so proud of their castle, would relish that ambition.

# Pardon My Molière

*By Jeffrey Forrester*

**Artwork by Tod Machin**

What do Molière and "The Addams Family" have in common? Not much, you might say at first glance. But further examination reveals a number of incredible similarities between the works of the seventeenth-century playwright and the 1960s television series.

1. Both were more or less critically underappreciated in their day.
2. Both showcased caricatures of so-called "deviate" personalities within the context of outrageous farce.
3. Both were funny.

It is that last point, perhaps, that made both the plays of Molière and the teleplays of "The Addams Family" popular with the masses. And it could very well be that single most important aspect of comedy—whether or not it makes you laugh—that damned both bodies of work to at least contemporary critical neglect.

But while the clever Frenchman was eventually recognized by his countrymen for his artistic genius (even though he was certainly no Jerry Lewis), the Family Addams still more or less languishes in relative ignominy. Such is the fate of some of the funniest TV shows in the history of the medium. One need only to examine the status of "Green Acres," another mid-sixties sitcom, for proof. Here was a program so clever, so ahead of its time, and so belly-laugh hilarious that its very hilariousness excluded it from anything but cursory appraisal. Sure, it was weird—that's why it was great. Virtually the same argument could be made for "The Addams Family."

During its original network run, "The Addams Family" was lumped with shows like "The Munsters" as just another cornball costume comedy cashing in on kids' fascination with monsters and creepy characters. But while "The Munsters" was essentially a straightforward Stupid Dad comedy (the twist being that Dad was Frankenstein's Monster), "The Addams Family" was highly original and brilliantly inventive in both premise and execution. It *was* creepy and kooky, mysterious and spooky, altogether "ooky." The mere fact that the show's composer and lyricist, Vic Mizzy, had the chutzpah to invent a new word because nothing else rhymed with "spooky" and "kooky" told you right off the bat this show had no intentions of following established sitcom rules. In fact, making up a word to fit a lyric was probably the only easy out that ever surfaced on "The Addams Family."

And that brings us to perhaps the most distinguishable aspect of the show: the scripts. Supervised by the legendary Nat Perrin (who also produced), they were fast-moving and literate. In most contemporary TV comedy, "fast-moving" and "literate" make for strange bedfellows; sitcoms seem to be either just fast-moving (like "Who's the Boss?") or just literate (like "Molly Dodd"). Producer Perrin was known for his professional association with the Marx Brothers, who were also fast-moving *and* literate, so perhaps the fact that "The Addams Family" shared those qualities was by no means accidental.

Another interesting aspect of the "Addams Family" teleplays was that every line was a laugh line. The same might be said of "The Dick

Van Dyke Show," for example; but Rob Petrie and company lived in a real world where the audience would take for granted much of the comedic premises. "The Addams Family," on the other hand, was bizarre from the word "go." One can imagine that wringing laughter from individually peculiar characters, set against a distinctly peculiar backdrop, was devilishly hard work. I can only surmise that the most easily written "Addams Family" scenes were those that involved "normal" characters attempting to deal with the goofy family. At least then the scriptwriter had a backboard of contrast for the characters to bounce off of.

In a sense, the show had nothing going for it and everything going for it. The "nothing" part was that by the sheer gimmicky nature of its premise, it was almost certain to be dismissed as hokum, however unjustifiably. The "everything" part extended to literally all other aspects of the show's makeup. In addition to the writing, "The Addams Family" was interesting *looking,* unique in flavor, and gloriously imaginative. Above all, it was passionate. When the kids were at play, they meant business. They didn't just pretend to dynamite a wing of the house—they *really did it.* Uncle Fester relieved his headaches by sticking his dome into a vise and having someone tighten it until it "popped," orgasmlike. Grandmama wrestled alligators and threw knives with lip-licking abandon. Even stoic Lurch played the harpsichord with an all-consuming intensity that approached sexual delight. And of course the relationship between Gomez and Morticia was the stuff dreams are made of ("Tish, that's French!"). A perfect blending of unconditional love and red-hot passion, it was the first—and only—relationship of its kind ever depicted on the tube. Sometimes, their individually smoldering sensuality extended beyond their marital relationship. In one classic scene, Morticia asks an attractive neighbor couple if they would object to her smoking. When the husband says they wouldn't mind, Morticia folds her arms and glares at them, vamplike, while wisps of smoke curl up around her torso. This apparent hint at a ménage à trois is perhaps one of the funniest dirty jokes ever presented on television, yet it was decidedly harmless because of the basically innocent nature of the character. In the hands of virtually any other sitcom mom, the gag would have played lascivious; with Morticia, it was natural.

Perhaps another reason "The Addams Family" is ignored is that essentially, it looked *too* natural. Laurel and Hardy suffered a similar fate; so relaxed were Stan and Ollie in their performances that even many contemporary critics continue to dismiss them as talented laugh getters rather than the intuitive geniuses they were. The players of "The Addams Family" were similarly fated. John Astin *was* Gomez, Carolyn Jones *was* Morticia, and Jackie Coogan seemingly *was* Uncle Fester. As an ensemble comedy, the show was perfectly cast, sublimely integrated, and brilliantly performed. There is a rumor going around that the cast was genuinely fond of each other, itself an anomaly in the annals of situation comedy. But I'd like to believe it, because the characters themselves radiated tolerance, compassion, and, most important of all, love.

The "love" aspect may have been what really put "The Addams Family" over with audiences. The average fan might say he likes the show because it's imaginative and funny-creepy, but more likely it's because the characters really love each other, and love their fellow man as well. The humanism is just played out against a horror-film background. For all their inherent bizarreness, they were probably the nicest family in all of sixties television.

In the long run, that's why the show may have had such extraordinary appeal to kids. I was in kindergarten when "The Addams Family" aired prime-time, and I was almost consumed with affection for it. In fact, I was once reprimanded for slipping the characters' names into the Pledge of Allegiance. If memory serves me, it went something like ". . . and to Uncle Fester, for which it stands, one Addams Family, under Gomez, invisible, with Pugsley and Wednesday for all." (I always thought I added "invisible" mainly to tip my hat to the Invisible Man; but let's face it—there's not a five-year-old anywhere who could tell you what the hell "indivisible" means, let alone pronounce it.)

In retrospect, it's easy to see other reasons "The Addams Family" is so embraced by children. What kid between the ages of three and thirteen wouldn't like to ride a motorcycle down the stairs or have a trampoline set up in the living room? Or blow up model trains, dynamite his bedroom, or put a spoiled playmate's head into a guillotine? Personally, I always got a charge when Pugsley or Wednesday was able to frighten—innocently, of course—the truant officer or some other pompous adult authority figure. I envied their power to make grown-ups quake with fear, and I think many other kids must have gotten the same kick.

Despite the love of millions upon millions of both kid and adult fans, the show was canned after only two seasons, even though "The Addams Family" was occasionally beating NBC's "Bob Hope Presents the Chrysler Theater" in the ratings. The fact that the Square One moved to a different time slot to avoid competition from the hip Family should have told ABC they had a good thing going; but CBS's "The Munsters" was declining in the ratings, and apparently ABC felt "The Addams Family" would follow.

As a result, we've got only two seasons' worth of "The Addams Family" to enjoy in reruns. But like those sterling half-hour "Honeymooners," they are treasured indeed, not only because the "Addams" episodes were top-notch farce, but because they represent a truly original moment in television history, and most of the performers who brought it to grim life are long dead: there will be no more "Addams Family" original-cast reunions, ever, and that notion may be grimmer than anything presented on this beloved program.

In retrospect, I guess, one could argue the Addamses don't really share much in common with Molière. But from one point of view, "The Addams Family" may have *bested* him. In terms of sheer productivity, at least, they've probably got him nailed. I don't know how long it took the playwright to crank out something like *The Misanthrope,* but I'm pretty sure he wasn't doing it thirty-five times a year. As for cultural influence, it's pretty doubtful anyone ever bothered to market anything like a *Misanthrope* coloring book, while "Addams Family" collectibles can still be exhumed in nostalgia shops throughout the world. And most significantly, from the aspect of overall audience appeal, well, "The Addams Family" would seem to win that one hands down. There probably isn't a kid alive who doesn't hate Molière—who, after all, never treated his fans to anything as daring or liberating as having a character ride a motorcycle down a flight of stairs with a light bulb in his mouth. All things considered, perhaps the only thing "The Addams Family" really shared with Molière was a passion for funny costumes.

But as the playwright himself might have put it, *"C'est la passion."* Molière! That's French!

AUTHOR'S NOTE: Jeff Forrester's fascination with "The Addams Family" apparently resulted in the permanent warping of his psyche. The Los Angeles–based producer recently received the Best Fiction Production award from the American Film Institute for *They're Still Breathing,* a comedy film about a man obsessed with "so-called dead celebrities," ranging from Elvis and Jim Morrison to Jack Webb and Shemp of the Three Stooges. The film, hosted by Harry Anderson, is slated for release by MPI Home Video in 1991; Forrester's release is still pending.

# The Family Fortune

*We Addamses have not worked in three hundred years—supervised and managed, yes . . . but worked, never!*

*—GOMEZ ADDAMS*

 Ever wonder exactly *what* Gomez did for a living, or how the Addamses amassed so much money? It was all by fair play, I'm sure. They were too honest to gain funds by any other means. Well, most of them—Fester might shoot someone in the back if the situation called for it.

So how did Gomez accumulate drawers full of "petty cash" which he generously handed out at whim? Why did cash fill every nook in the house, with plenty more in the kitchen? ("The big stuff's upstairs in the mattress," Gomez explained.) And how was the family able to play at home with no visible means of support?

Of course, these riddles are among the unanswered mysteries that surround Skipper and Gilligan's "three-hour tour" and the accompanying Howell fortune aboard the S.S. *Minnow.* And the vast wardrobe . . . and the Professor's science texts, etc.

As Addams lore has it, Gomez "Loophole" Addams was a nonpracticing attorney who held the record for sending the most criminals to jail—not as prosecuting attorney but as counsel in their defense. Gomez retired from the bar after he scored a fortune from investments. He regularly inspected his antique, glass-domed stock ticker in the living room and investigated the stock reports in the newspapers— while standing on his head. Among his many real estate holdings,

*Courtesy of John Astin*

Gomez owned a mango plantation (located next to a colony of cannibals), a crocodile farm in Mozambique, tapioca mines on top of Mount Everest, and a nut farm in Brazil. The Addamses also owned controlling interest in Excelsior Corporations, which owned the insurance companies covering the family (e.g., the Arthur J. Henson Insurance Company).

For the business-minded, the eager students of finance, and even the casual investor, Gomez shared two formulas for success:

1. "Addams Law (. . . otherwise known as How to Slit Your Competitor's Throat Without Getting Blood on His Necktie): Simple rule—when selling off, never accept the first nine offers. When they come up with number ten—grab it!"
2. "I've got it! We'll invent something that costs a dime to make—sell it for a dollar—and is habit-forming."

## THE MASTER PLAN

GOMEZ: I'll set him up in his own business. I'll capitalize it at five hundred thousand dollars and amortize the principle over a ten-year period.

MORTICIA: Darling, what does that mean?

GOMEZ: Who knows? That's the way I run all my enterprises.

# Dining for the Deranged

*Can you imagine roast aardvark without an apple in its mouth? It's like a martini without the egg.*
                                    —*GOMEZ ADDAMS*

## "BON APPETIT!"

These delectable entrees constitute the Addamses' daily diets:

baked iguana
baked mongoose      *blackbird pie (Things ruined it - he let them get away. All 24 of them.)*
braised giraffe
braised lion loin
breast of alligator
broiled elephant hooves      *buzzard broth      Candied porcupine*
casserole of spleen (with a pinch of hemlock)
casserole of yak      *('Not like yak? you make them sound weird.')*
cup of hot sea sludge (dessert)
dwarf's-hair cobbler
eye of newt (baked)
eye of tadpole (a delicacy; substitute for caviar)
flambé of jellyfish (mistaken for cherries jubilee)
fricassee of toad      *giraffe burger (for Cleopatra)*
gopher goulash
gopher loaf
henbane soup

*Bat broth*

*horse*
*instant yak - toasted!*

*" fillet of ferny-snake,*
*eye of newt" etc*

44

marinated gizzard of lizard — ("au crouton") *pâté of yak*

*Salamander puffs ("rich desserts")*

pinecone nectar (perfect beverage)

puree of sea sludge

*Scorpion paté on fresh toadstools —*

soufflé of aardvark

*with belladonna sauce // porcupine taffy*

toadstool soufflé

tongue of yak ("Fresh. It costs more than the quick-frozen,
    but it's so much tastier," says Morticia)

tripe of salamander ("Perfect for breakfast," says Gomez)

yak fudge

*yak stew — "I shot the yak myself!" — Mama*

*yak gravy on mutton bread (just gluten — "Not the way he* ate it!"

## QUOTATIONS

MORTICIA (*serving guests*): "Salt, pepper, or cyanide?" *(in the wolfbane tea)*

Fester's recipe for fudge: Sulfur, charcoal, and saltpeter . . . BOOM!
("Funny, I coulda sworn it made fudge.")

*~ Papa*

MORTICIA: "A watched cauldron never bubbles."

*A rare, behind-the-scenes snap, as the cast waits for the next shot to be filmed. Notice Morticia is not wearing the spider braids at the end of her dress (they clipped on). (Courtesy of Howard Frank)*

# Optically Speaking

 Did you every wonder *where* the old Addams mansion was located? A tour of Hollywood homes will leave you questioning, because the original structure used for exterior shots in the pilot presentation and the opening of each show (behind Gomez, while he files the gate prongs) has been razed. But this stately old mansion originally stood tall on Adams Boulevard in Los Angeles.

To shave the costs of constructing an actual full-scale front or the shell of a home, Filmways Productions devised a way to illustrate the rickety Addams house using a matte painting which was altered for moods. Howard Anderson II of the Howard Anderson Company, a film and television special effects team, hired artist Louis McMannus (the artist who designed TV's coveted Emmy Award) to paint a replica of the mansion filmed for the pilot presentation. The matte would be photographed as day, and altered for night, or stormy weather, by matting in opticals or painting in the light in a window or clouds up above. This "bumper," as it's sometimes called, was shown in between scenes—say, right after a commercial break.

Here's how the matte was constructed: A photograph of the original home on Adams Boulevard was blown up to a thirty-by-forty-inch black-and-white portrait. Artist McMannus brushed color oil paint over the photograph and added details and style to the home, such as a bent television antenna and bare trees. Stock footage was then shot of the house for day scenes, night scenes, gloomy weather, with lights shining from the windows, and the rest. Special effects, such as Pugsley's rockets launched from the attic into the night, were added in the post-

*The original matte painting of the Addams mansion (Courtesy of the Howard Anderson Company)*

production process. For each change, McMannus painted over the existing matte portrait. Today, that classic painting has disintegrated, says Anderson.

Additionally, Anderson's company produced the trademark and highly inventive "wipes"—the intrusive scene transitions such as fading, or dissolving, or cutting to another shot. An odd array of wipes such as exploding polka dots, an unraveling spiral, a shamrock that opens, starbursts, and circles that iris in and iris out, were optically inserted to guide viewers from one scene to another. "Those opticals were left over from the silent days," reveals Anderson. "My dad, who started the company in 1927, had a library of wipes, and we revamped them for the show. Not many programs used wipes like these." Truly a bizarre collection of eclectic visuals, these silent-picture leftovers— black-and-white to boot—perfectly complemented the Addams style. Later, these effects were popularized on TV's "Get Smart!"

The Anderson Company also produced titles and effects for other TV shows, such as "The Beverly Hillbillies," "Mr. Ed," and "Rin Tin

Tin." Its most recognizable work, however, must be the original "I Love Lucy" opening, with the familiar heart over a sheet of wrinkled satin. In 1966, Gene Roddenberry tapped the company to arrange the orbital optics for TV's original "Star Trek" pilot and the first ten episodes. "We had to quit after that because we couldn't keep up with the rigorous schedule," Anderson says. "That show involved quite a bit of time."

The Anderson Company, which at the time of "The Addams Family" was located on the lot of General Service Studios, now operates on the Universal Studios lot under the supervision of Howard Anderson III.

# The Family Secret: Formula for Success

*The props are first rate, but the people are even better. Beautiful Carolyn Jones plays Morticia with a chilling verve that should make any dead-blooded man want to share a bier with her.*
*—Time, December 3, 1964*

 Nat Perrin believes he knows exactly why the Addamses were so appealing. There are endless reasons why audiences clung to the Family and welcomed them into their homes each week; but as Perrin indicates, there was a truly unparalleled quality about this family that made you giggle and shudder deliciously. "There was *never*, in all of the episodes, a quarrel between Gomez and Morticia," he says. "I was aware, too, that this quality made the show more difficult to do, because fighting and calling somebody a meathead—there's a lot of comedy in that sort of conflict. I didn't have conflict, and it was a difficult way to produce comedy. When you had an outsider, yes, in the beginning it was a source of extra comedy. But how many times can you have the same reaction?"

He continues: "Of a thousand shows with husbands and wives, there was always bickering or misunderstandings. I didn't want to do another version of 'The Bickersons,' because I thought it would look like every other show."

Claiming the distinction of being the nicest family on television, the show subconsciously attracted a legion of fans, particularly children. What kids didn't dig this laid-back atmosphere? In one episode, for instance, the school principal vouches, "I'm sure your children will be

very happy here." Gomez retorts, "If we'd wanted them to be happy, we would've let them stay at home." And when they did stay at home, they were allowed to experiment with all types of odd playthings, animals, and normally forbidden materials such as TNT.

With the Addams Family on a popularity pedestal during their prime-time run, one incident impressed Nat Perrin the most. "One of the nicest, most flattering things happened," he says. "A psychiatrist from a newspaper who wrote a column said the best show on the air for children, by far, was 'The Addams Family.' He went on to say why: There wasn't the bickering. There wasn't the making a fool of the father or the mother. There weren't sides drawn between the children and their parents. There was all love, and they still managed to be funny.

"I was very proud of that," Perrin confesses with a wide smile.

Supporting this theory, Dr. Stephen Fried, Ph.D, head of the psychology department at Park College in Kansas City, Missouri, explains the phenomenon in this way: "Individuals in 'The Addams Family' were loved and accepted regardless of their behavior. Unconditional positive regard—that was unusual. The value judgments that were a very clear part of television then—right, wrong, good, bad—didn't seem so much in play in 'The Addams Family.' [There was] a genuine warmth . . . between the characters."

A different school of thought places the show's appeal among adults in the hands of a recurring, albeit unestablished, topic on television in the 1960s: sex. With "The Addams Family," it was never really sex per se, although there were a few lines, scattered innuendos, and of course the bursting flurry of romance between Gomez and Morticia in nearly every episode. Any utterance of a French phrase threw Gomez into a mild—sometimes wild—frenzy of passion. As he kissed his wife's arm all the way to her neck (sometimes he appeared to be licking her), he'd beg for more French. "You are a gem," he'd say. "And a tasty one, too."

"At that particular time, we got away with murder on a sexual basis," Herb Browar says regarding Gomez's unbridled lust. "When we cut away, he was still kissing her up the arm. If we had let the shot run, he could've gone on around and kissed her right on the tits!" And with Carolyn Jones "it was very tempting," laughs Nat Perrin. "It never got lewd, though. You could tell the intentions of the people. It never was

*Reprinted with permission from* **TV Guide**® *magazine,* © *1964 News America Publications, Inc., Radnor, PA*

## SAMPLING OF GOMEZ'S LOVE POETRY TO MORTICIA

When the blazing sun has turned to mud
And the moon lies dead in a pool of blood
And the tom-tom beat of eternity starts ...
Whom will I love in my heart of hearts?

Morticia!

When I first saw you from afar,
My heart flamed with fierce passion.
And when you spoke French, ooh-la-la,
Ah, your radiant beauty, your captivating allure,
Drew me to you like honey to a suckle.

intended to suggest sex—just great romance. It was so flamboyant. We never had much trouble."

During the sixties, network censors and executives were beginning gingerly to relax their mandates, but still Jeannie concealed the navel that men dreamed of. Pretty, homespun Kansas farm girl Mary Ann on "Gilligan's Island" was forced to hike her hip-huggers to hide her belly button. Until this era, in which the views of censors—and thus of audiences—were sometimes drastically altered, clean-cut "Father Knows Best" and "Leave It to Beaver" types were cluttering the market and tiring television tuners. "We knew all the families on TV at that time were antiseptic," laughs John Astin. "We felt it was time to have a normal, well-adjusted family—a husband and wife who actually could have had the children."

On a scale, Astin says fans most readily recall the passion, the French, and Thing. Buffs of the show still approach Astin, as Ringo Starr once did, spilling random French phrases and expecting an un-

## Terms of Interment—er, Endearment

*Gomez, I've been yours since that first day you*
*carved my initials in your leg.*
### —MORTICIA

Oddly, besides the far-flung French, Gomez reacted wildly
to Tish's crazy impression of a bullfrog—a sort of vocal
burp that Carolyn Jones had a knack for doing. Gomez affectionately called Morticia pet names such as "Querida" or
"Cara Mia," both being generic mating calls. In return,
Morticia would prompt his Latin love by calling her husband
"Bubeleh" or reciting random French. A smidgen from Morticia's discursive language of love:

> au revoir (goodbye)
> La Plume de Ma Tante (the pen of my aunt; also Tony
>     Award–winning Broadway musical)
> crêpes Suzette (flaming pancakes)
> Moulin Rouge (French nightclub)
> ooh-la-la (woo, woo)
> pâté de foie gras (goose-liver spread)
> mon ami (my friend)
> je ne sais quoi (I don't know what)
> vive la France (long live France)
> tour de force (a hard task)
> comme ci, comme ça (so-so)
> oui, oui (yes, yes)
> bon soir (good night)
> soupe du jour (soup of the day)

tested reaction. Ringo even grabbed Astin's arm and emulated Gomez. Astin stopped him at the elbow.

The association of Gomez's blazing flutter with French prompted at least one memorable letter. "[It] came in from some man in Virginia with six or seven kids," recalls Astin, smiling. "He said, 'Please have Gomez Addams confine his sexual activities to the bedroom.' That was rare."

Astin expounded, "I think we had a healthy attitude about it. We were playing a husband and wife truly in love with one another. As I look back on it, Carolyn and I never spoke of it. Both of us had an idealistic attitude toward marriage. Carolyn had a marriage that wasn't working out, and I, too, had some marital problems. Both of us really wanted a good marriage, and both of us really loved our mates at the time. Each of us probably wished we could have a marriage free of problems, and both of us played that out in the show. I know I did. I rather think Carolyn did too."

# Smoke Screams

*Here, have a cigar. Light it up and be somebody!*
                                    —Pete Kelly's Blues

"The Addams Family" is like a fine cigar.

Why? I have no idea. Someone once said it, and it may bear repeating. Maybe Gomez said it. There *is* a nexus, you know. A good cigar lingers, just as the Addamses. Sometimes a cigar stinks—like a few clinkers in the Addams batch. In fact, one of the sponsors of the show was Consolidated Cigar Corporation, points out John Astin. And in the wisdom of Morticia Addams, a cigar, like brandy after dinner, is "a sign of sophistication and culture." The show reeked of culture and sophistication.

Regardless, cigar aficionado that Gomez was, there remains a bond between the fine art of smoking a stogie and relaxing to an unrelentingly oddball episode of the Addamses. Someone also said, "Cigars are like cats—fit for indoors, in a comfortable armchair next to a cozy fire in the winter, near an open window in the summer. But avoid both the radiator and the air conditioning." How true. That also bore repeating.

In his book, *Holy Smoke,* G. Cabrera Infante revels in the art of finding, rolling, smoking, and discussing the rolled gold. He cites authors, politicians, world leaders, actors, and other celebrities. The notorious smokers discussed include Sigmund Freud, Winston Churchill, Mark Twain, Sir Walter Raleigh, W. C. Fields, Groucho Marx, even Lou Costello and the Three Stooges. Orson Welles, a man who once said that he made movies to be able to smoke cigars for free, is quoted: "That's why I write so many cigar-smoking heroes and villains who

chomp their cigars," he declared. "Cigars are my inspiration. The bigger, the better then." Infante, whose favorite film smoker is Edward G. Robinson, also reminisces about small-screen smokers like George Burns, Ernie Kovacs ("the television comedian who smoked the most aggressive, ostentatious, and fattest Havanas"), and Milton Berle. But he forgot one: Gomez Addams.

Gomez was a smoker from way back, but rarely did you actually see him torch his everlasting García y Vegas. (He sometimes lit a match off Lurch's palm, or Thing flicked a lighter for him. Fester once flared the cigar with his flame blower.) Even the bride and groom atop Gomez and Morticia's wedding cake featured a miniature Gomez puffing away. His life centered around his cigars, which were always long and lit, never a stub. Gomez enjoyed them to a fault. Like George Burns, he used them as a prop. He spoke with them, fondled them, and punctuated his speech with them like an appropriate comma in a sentence.

William Makepeace Thackeray, who called tobacco "that kindly weed," said of cigars:

> Honest men with . . . cigars in their mouths, have great physical advantages in conversation. You may stop talking if you like—but the breaks of silence never seem disagreeable, being fueled up by the puffing of the smoke. . . . The cigar harmonizes society, and soothes at once the speaker and the subject whereon he converses. I have no doubt that it is from the habit of smoking that . . . American Indians are such monstrous well-bred men.

Havana or not, like most politicians, Gomez *was* well spoken and well bred, with a deep Addams background in history. Moreover, in one memorable episode, Gomez decided to run for mayor; his campaign slogan proudly pronounced on posters: "Gomez for Mayor: Watch His Smoke!" He routinely placed lit cigars in his suit pocket—never igniting threads, of course. His cigar-store Indian standing sternly in the living room always stocked a handful. (This prop was similar to the Indian on TV's "Cheers," which guards the bar's door like a beloved mascot.) A passionate smoker, Gomez truly loved his cigar almost as much as he loved his wife.

Morticia never opposed the cigar smoke that wafted around the room like haunting spirits. After all, *she* smoked—her whole body evoked a mushroom cloud on cue. Among many favorite household items, there was a Chinese gold dragon which she affectionately patted, prompting bursts of smoke to shoot from its nostrils in satisfaction. It was almost alive.

*Holy Smoke* adds, "Groucho [Marx] with his cigar did to comedy what the other Marx [Karl] with his cheroot did to economy: revolutionize it and in so doing destroy order, hierarchy and rules. It's all there in *Das Kapital* and *Duck Soup.*" Didn't the Addams Family abolish those same rules—*any* rules? They didn't pretend to fit in society. They assumed they were model citizens.

The legendary Groucho, rarely seen without a cigar in hand, either had a Punch in his mouth or a pun. Maybe the same can be said of Gomez Addams. Critic Mark Dawidziak wrote, "As the head of the

*Similarities abound between Groucho and Gomez. (Courtesy of Howard Frank Archives)*

household, he was like Groucho Marx, with manic energy, puffing away wildly on the cigar, eyes rolling around. He was the keeper of the asylum."

Similarities between the Family Addams and the Brothers Marx extend beyond mere tobacco. Producer, writer, and director Nat Perrin cut his teeth in the business writing for the Marx Brothers, garnering screen credit for *Duck Soup* and *The Big Store*. Perrin fueled Groucho with material for many years, became close friends with the comedian, and was named his estate's conservator in the rocky end of the late comedian's legacy.

Perrin's style shone through his "Addams" scripts and scenes, sometimes—consciously or not—creating a Marx Brothers routine between Fester, Morticia, and Gomez. The same off-the-wall, left-field comedy distinguished both Marxes and Addamses. Perrin concedes:

"Gomez was played a great deal like Groucho," he says. "The writing came out that way, in my style."

John Astin, however, having created Gomez (with a cigar) before Perrin joined the production, never strove to imitate Marx. "Gomez came out of me," Astin points out. "I smoked cigars at the time and thought it would be right for the character—like growing a mustache. I lit so many of those things on the show, including off the set, that I finally quit after 'Addams Family.' I remember when the show came out, people compared me to Groucho Marx, Peter Sellers, and Ernie Kovacs," he adds with a grin. "I mentioned this to Nat Perrin one day. He said, 'My boy, they're all good. Don't worry about it.' "

'Aristotle'

B. DAVIS

# Creepers and Crawlers

*Anyone who hates an octopus is warped.*
—GOMEZ ADDAMS

Didn't every little schoolboy have a pet octopus in the 1960s? Pugsley Addams did, and he named it Aristotle. Little Wednesday's pet tarantula was named Homer, and she was also fond of Lucifer, a salamander that slithered around her neck. ✗

The largest pet the Addamses befriend was their feline cuddle Kitty Kat, a full-grown African lion that roamed the house with no restrictions. Animal trainer Steve Martin, who "worked" some of the beasts on the "Addams" set, raised the lion from a cub. Sometimes he'd affix a leash and walk it onto the set; but occasionally he rode the lion onto the soundstage. Mostly, stock footage of the lion walking down the main stairs or growling into the camera was reused, alleviating the lion's trips to the studio.

The family also kept a few less aggressive pets. If you remember, a piranha inhabited the fish tank, an alligator (which Uncle Fester wrestled), resided in the basement, and on a perch in the corner of the living room was the infamous Zelda.

The first, and only, sitcom vulture, Zelda was really named Old Granny by her guardian. Owned, trained, and loved by Darrel Keener, the vulture had come from the Andes Mountains in South America when it was a baby. It was nearly thirty years old when it appeared several times on "The Addams Family." Unrestrained and perched like an ordinary parakeet, this vulture would send a sudden screech that prompted astonished silence. Although the bird was gentle in nature, it

60

✗ Wednesday's chameleon - "that ghastly bug" - Gomez out of his mind

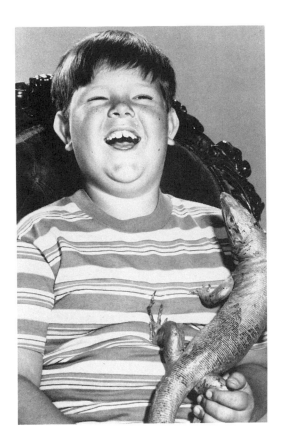

*Pugsley had the best pets in the world! (Personality Photos, Inc.)*

pecked at Carolyn Jones while filming one day, and the director left it in the episode because her reaction was so natural. Eventually, recalls director of photography Archie Dalzell, Jones became fond of the vulture and caressed it lovingly. "To listen to Carolyn talk to that old vulture was like baby talk to a love bird," he says.

"Although it was named Old Granny, I think it was a male vulture because of the loud red coloring," says longtime animal trainer Frank Inn. "The females weren't as pretty as the males. But this one had a wing span of about five feet. We kept it pretty fat, and it was probably too heavy to fly much, although we could fly it to a pedestal or back to us. It was very gentle with us on the show, and I used to let it sit on my arm. They don't grip as hard as a big hawk. And of course, an eagle's claws will clamp down and meet each other."

Frank Inn was the marvel trainer of such popular stars as Benji, Arnold the Pig on "Green Acres," Ol' Duke on "The Beverly Hillbillies,"

Animal trainer Frank Inn with his beloved Arnold the Pig, who made two appearances on "The Addams Family" (Courtesy of Frank Inn)

and many more lovable celluloid creatures. During the 1960s, he supplied animals to such General Service Studios TV shows as "The Adventures of Ozzie and Harriet" and "Petticoat Junction" as well as "The Beverly Hillbillies" and "Green Acres." Later, Inn used Old Granny the vulture in a 1976 film titled *Hawmps,* starring James Hampton and Jack Elam: if you watch closely, you can spot Granny sittin' atop an outhouse throughout.

Another of Inn's favorites was Arnold the Pig. One of the several young Arnolds crossed the studio lot and made two guest shots on "The Addams Family" as Pugsley's live piggy bank, whitewashed, with lettering on its side. Pugsley would chase the frightened piglet into the closet, closing the door behind them. The viewer heard scuffling, and anyone could imagine the chubby boy squeezing pennies from the pig. When the door opened, a smiling Pugsley sauntered out, rattling his change, and the pig peeked out, releasing a loud "Whew!" Poor Arnold probably hated the Addams Family: after all, in Hooterville he was royalty.

## MIDWEEK'S POEM

I have a gloomy little spider
I love to sit down close beside her.

She never knows where she has been
'Cause all she does is spin and spin.

My spider's quite a busy roamer,
Which is why I called her Homer.

She loves to work and spin all day,
And then at night she likes to play.

Her web is like my mother's hair,
Her eyes have got my father's stare.

She may not jump or twist or bend,
But a spider is a girl's best friend.

BY WEDNESDAY ADDAMS

# Up and Addams

*Every day is a party with us.*
*—MORTICIA ADDAMS*

 Because the Addams clan had no responsibilities whatsoever, the family had time to devote to the eccentric activities they enjoyed most. These pastimes were as unusual as the family itself, but seemingly fitting. The Addamses occupied themselves with zestful fun, with never a dull moment in the house. Curiously, this all-American family plopped in front of the boob tube only twice in all the episodes, and maybe listened to the radio once. They were old-fashioned in their spirits and needed only themselves and their playthings to be entertained.

As amusing as most of their activities were, Morticia actually commented once, "We do lead such routine lives." But at any time, day or night (they preferred a compromise: a gloomy, rainy day), you may witness the Family intensely consumed with any one of the following activities:

• Gomez and Morticia often enjoyed smoking from a genuine Turkish hookah together. No one knows *what* they smoked. After all, this *was* the sixties.
• The entire family enjoyed moonbathing in their backyard with a picniclike atmosphere. Gomez sported an old, striped swimsuit; and they all wore protective sun gear, while Fester used the moon-burn lotion (he literally consumed it—"Whaddaya want me to do—smear it all over my face?").

In their "outing" garb, ready to moonbathe and enjoy a picnic (Milton Moore Collection)

• Any number of sports were set up in the living room: badminton, volleyball, croquet, spear chucking. Occasionally, Gomez enjoyed a good spring on a monstrous trampoline.

• Morticia enjoyed knitting: her projects included a two-headed ski cap for Cousin Plato and a three-armed sweater for Cousin Imar. (Carolyn Jones actually knitted in her spare time.)

• Uncle Fester's penchant for blasting a cannon inside the house caused repairmen to be summoned on several occasions. His use of a flame thrower disintegrated Smokey, the family's stuffed bear, in a later episode.

• Gomez's favorite soothing diversion was pursuing his fetish for electric trains. He destroyed the trains by crashing them and detonating charges at their collision point. (Filmways, in an effort to conserve funds, shot footage of a train wreck for the pilot presentation and reused this for almost every subsequent episode.)

• Morticia and Gomez enjoyed sword duels with real rapiers . . . "En garde!"

• Uncle Fester rode his motorcycle down the stairs and through the house. When he sulked, he retreated to his treehouse.

*Morticia feeding Cleopatra, her African Strangler plant (Personality Photos, Inc.)*

• Gomez is a member in good standing of the Zen Yogi Society, constantly practicing the entangled postures of yoga. "It's the only way to find inner peace," says Gomez, a true believer. (John Astin actually practiced yoga during the show; today he's a Buddhist.)

• Cleopatra, the overgrown African strangler plant, was Morticia's pet. She fed it large meatball-like treats, among other feasts for the carnivorous house plant. (An Addams version of *Little Shop of Horrors*?) Morticia also enjoyed gardening. She maintained a lovely grove of hemlock, henbane, and deadly nightshade. She clipped the rosebuds off their stems and left the thorn-bursting rods to create a wonderful stem bouquet.

• Grandmama enjoyed knife throwing as a relaxing sport, and whipping up such delicacies as yak stew in the kitchen.

- Lurch's love was playing music on his harpsichord.
- The children played most of the time, sometimes in lieu of school. Pugsley's favorite venture was experimenting with dynamite in the house; Uncle Fester would assist.

## A TYPICAL GOMEZ TELEPHONE CONVERSATION

"Hello, Mr. Hulen? Addams here. I just called to tell you that I'm taking my family on a nice, long cruise. We're going to gather some fish for our children's collection—new ones! Have to go deeper and deeper, you know. So would you be a good chap and run out and buy us a submarine? With nuclear power, of course . . . Mr. Hulen? . . . HULEN?"

# "I'm Gomez...He's Fester"

 John Astin arrived in Hollywood in 1960 thanks to a push from his friend Tony Randall. His first motion picture role was Gladhand, the social worker in *West Side Story,* which eventually led to a string of work on television. Just prior to "The Addams Family," in 1962–63, he co-starred with Marty Ingels in the nearly forgotten Leonard Stern sitcom "I'm Dickens . . . He's Fenster" on ABC.

Before accepting the role of Gomez Addams, Astin—who carefully contemplates all his work—thought to himself, "Why do people watch television?" and "What do they want?"

"At that time, I felt people watch to live some kind of dream," says Astin of the medium. "Maybe to reaffirm values. I thought my next character would be one a great number of the audience could identify with. I would move toward specific goals as a character that would affirm humanistic views, because I felt then, and I still do, that we live in a world that behaves in a barbaric manner much of the time.

"But human beings, inside, actually crave humanism," Astin says. "They want to love one another and have an appreciation of the beauty of life. So I determined [my] next character would express this. My good fortune was [that] the producer, David Levy, was open to ideas like this and willing to let the character develop." Surely the actor's goals were met in his portrayal of Gomez Addams, the role for which he probably is best remembered.

Astin takes great pride in his theater work, which preceded the series and continues today. His training was in Shakespeare and other classical dramatists. As understudy for a leading role in Charles Laugh-

A Christmas publicity photo of the John Astin family in 1965, with wife, Suzanne, and sons David, Thomas, and Allen (Courtesy of John Astin)

John and Patty Duke Astin in the 1970s (Courtesy of John Astin)

ton's Broadway production of Shaw's *Major Barbara,* he went on and stopped the show. He stunned audiences with a brilliant performance as Iago in *Othello* and appeared in New York in *The Threepenny Opera* and *Ulysses in Nighttown,* among other plays. His portrayal of Vladimir in *Waiting for Godot* won Astin rave reviews.

Astin did not always crave the greasepaint, however: his achievements in school suggest that he could have become a physicist rather than an actor. He showed an early aptitude for mathematics; he once mastered a semester's work in differential equations in one night.

The son of Margaret and Allen Astin, he was born in Baltimore, Maryland, on March 30, 1930. When he was less than a year old his family moved to Washington, D.C., where he attended Janney School, Bethesda Elementary School, and Woodrow Wilson High. With his skill with numbers, he earned a grant to attend Washington and Jefferson College, where he discovered an interest in drama. He transferred to Johns Hopkins University during his junior year and changed to a drama major, bringing down the curtain on math. Later, he attended graduate school in English literature at the University of Minnesota while partic-

*Photograph by Stephen Cox*

ipating in community theater and summer stock. Astin also attended the Greet Academy of Dramatic Arts in Washington, D.C., honing his would-be professional skills. Later, in New York, he studied for five years under theater master Harold Clurman, who founded The Group Theater.

When his legitimate stage work led to films and television in California, his new home base, Astin was married to Suzanne Hahn, a red-headed actress who was also in the cast of *The Threepenny Opera;* they had three children. They were divorced after the "Addams Family" run. In 1972 he married another actress, Patty Duke, with whom he had two more children. Astin and Duke had lived together for a few years prior to their marriage, which lasted until 1985. During their marriage, John and Patty Duke toured as a theatrical team, breaking attendance records, sometimes being compared to the Lunts and the Barrymores. Happily remarried, he and his present wife, Valerie, currently live in Los Angeles.

Astin keeps in theatrical shape by performing in one play per year if he can. His alter ego Gomez Addams precedes him wherever he goes, however. It's no wonder that this role is his most recognized, since the "Addams" merchandising line during the 1960s painted his face on a myriad of items. "The network made big deals for merchandising, and you end up with supposedly 5 percent of the profits," explains Astin. "They could sell millions worth of this stuff, but there were never any profits. It's strange at best that of all the stuff that was sold, I probably made between two hundred fifty and five hundred dollars. There were Halloween masks, Gomez this, Gomez that, card games, toys—zillions of things."

Another portrayal that won him recognition, laughs, and a cult status was the title character in the TV film *Evil Roy Slade,* which still airs on late-night television occasionally. If it were shown in prime time today, it would be a hit, the actor maintains. Astin starred in the TV series "Operation Petticoat" (1977–1978) based on the 1959 film.

Still, Astin favors the "Addams" experience as something he would not trade—except for the time the script called for him to peek up the chimney and speak to Cousin Itt. An incorrectly timed burst of soot caked his wide-open eyes, and filming was halted for an hour while the makeup man carefully rinsed his eyelids and pupils. "It took every ounce of concentration I could muster not to blink," he recalled. "Oh, that was hell. My mother happened to be on the set that day, and she got pretty nervous."

The same weight now as when he starred as Gomez, Astin stays fit and continues a vegetarian diet. He directs and continues writing (his tragi-comic featurette *Prelude* reaped an Academy Award nomination for best short subject), and works in films and television, including voice-over work for commercials and animated cartoons. He has finished filming *Attack of the Killer Tomatoes, Part IV,* reprising his role as Dr. Gangrene from the preceding installments. And as a running character on TV's "Night Court," he played Judge Stone's father, Buddy Ryan, an outlandish kook with a familiar strain of Gomez Addams.

### Additional Movie Appearances

*That Touch of Mink; The Wheeler Dealers; Move Over Darling; Candy; Viva Max; Pepper; Get to Know Your Rabbit; Two on a Bench; The Dream Makers; The Brothers O'Toole; Only with Married Men; Skyway to Death; The Spirit Is Willing; Every Little Crook and Nanny; Bad Day at Blue Nose; Operation Petticoat* (TV movie); *Freaky Friday; Teen Wolf Too; National Lampoon's European Vacation; Gremlins II; Nightlife; The Blue Dulac.*

### Additional Television Appearances

"Kraft Playhouse"; "Philco Playhouse"; "Armstrong Circle Theater"; "The Donna Reed Show"; "Route 66"; "The Gertrude Berg Show"; "The Farmer's Daughter"; "Destry"; "The Phyllis Diller Show"; "Batman"; "Hey Landlord"; "Sheriff Who"; "The Flying Nun"; "Gunsmoke"; "He and She"; "The Doris Day Show"; "CBS Playhouse"; "Bonanza"; "Love, American Style"; "Night Gallery"; "The Odd Couple"; "The Partridge Family"; "Peter Loves Mary"; "Welcome Back, Kotter"; "Temperatures Rising"; "McMillan and Wife"; "Holmes and Yoyo"; "Mary"; "Love Boat"; "Fantasy Island"; "Murder, She Wrote."

# Delicia Morticia

Her limelight began when she played a lonely Greenwich Village existentialist in the movie *The Bachelor Party* in 1957. Her sizzling, six-minute portrayal snared her an Academy Award nomination, which took her by surprise because, she later admitted, she never understood the role.

Carolyn Jones in 1982, just a year before her death, spoke of her Oscar nomination with *Hollywood Drama-Logue* reporter Pat Broeske: "The original script had my character saying lines like, 'My martini has no olives, the scotch no rocks,' " Jones recalled of the beatnik role. The peppery actress "had the gall" to tell scriptwriter Paddy Chayefsky she couldn't understand the character whatsoever. "She was one of those Greenwich Village intellectual dummies," said Jones of the character she portrayed. "I finally said to Paddy, 'You've got to get somebody else because I don't know how to play this part. I don't know a girl who would say lines like these.' "

Jones stayed with the production, and her now-famous line, "Just say you love me—you don't have to mean it," let the rest of her career roll.

Ever since she was a little girl in Texas, she had aimed at motion-picture stardom. The acting was part of it; but she fancied the look, the class, the whole image of "a star," which she gradually attained.

Carolyn Sue Jones was born in Amarillo on April 28, 1929 (inaccurate reports give 1933), of Comanche Indian ancestry. Always thin, she reached five foot five, and blossomed into a beautiful woman, with brilliantly blue eyes. Before starting her career, she was bent on changing her image. A *Los Angeles Times* article quoted her intentions:

*Starlet Carolyn Jones in the 1950s (World Wide Photos)*

"When I was growing up I was painfully thin," she admitted in 1964. "My posture was bad. My hair was so fine it would not keep a curl, and on top of all that I had acne." She later capped her teeth, had her nose fixed, dyed her hair from blond to brunet, and set out to take the studios by storm.

Her first professional acting exposure was at the Pasadena Community Playhouse, where she lied about her age to enroll in the summer stock series, she says. Just before graduation from the Pasadena school, she appeared in Tennessee Williams's *Summer and Smoke,* where she attracted the attention of a movie talent scout as well as Aaron Spelling, then a theater actor, writer, and director. Spelling soon cast her in *The Live Wire,* which he was directing at the Preston Sturges Players Theater in Hollywood.

Paramount Pictures lured Jones away from the theater to films, where she made her debut in *The Turning Point,* with William Holden, in 1952. This small role led to other films, including *Military Policeman* and the Bob Hope–Bing Crosby *Road to Bali* where she played a sexy

Australian. She captured a role in *House of Wax* with Vincent Price—in 3-D, no less—and performed with Marlon Brando in *Desiree,* Frank Sinatra in *The Tender Trap,* and James Stewart in *The Man Who Knew Too Much,* under Alfred Hitchcock's direction. Her associations with the Hollywood elite delighted her immensely; her childhood dream was coming true.

Cast as a glamorous vixen opposite Elvis Presley in *King Creole,* probably his most dramatic film (many fans claim it's his best), Jones dies in the arms of the King. "I had a temperature of 104 when we did those sequences. Boy, was I sick!" she said in 1964. "I kept saying, 'Elvis, don't kiss me. I'll give you something.' He kept telling me, 'Don't worry.' " Immediately following the picture, Elvis was off to the Army, and Jones remained his last screen kiss—for a while.

When they were filming *The Seven Year Itch,* her dressing room was across the hall from Marilyn Monroe's. The two would leave their

*Carolyn Jones and Aaron Spelling in 1964 arriving at the Cocoanut Grove in Hollywood. (World Wide Photos)*

*A sixties shot of Carolyn Jones with a glint in her eye (Courtesy of Howard Frank Archives)*

doors open to chat. "She was such a sad lady," remembered Jones. "She was just getting to the stage where she was frightened about losing her looks. It was an all-consuming fear."

Jones married Aaron Spelling on April 10, 1953. Over a decade later, she accepted her most famous role, the wickedly weird Morticia Addams, upon her husband's advice. At the time, Jones and Spelling lived in a two-hundred-thousand-dollar, all-white "old traditional Hollywood-style" mansion. Her closets were filled with furs, and her drawers shone from diamonds. Her clothes were specially designed, and she was starring in a network television show. Her life appeared perfect on the outside, but into the first season of the show, she and Spelling divorced, although they remained friendly.

Always one who "likes action," she told *TV Guide,* she threw Hollywood parties at her home, inviting the elite of Tinseltown. One such party she hosted during the "Addams" run had a Halloween theme, complete with costumed waiters and a guest of honor to beat 'em all: Charles Addams. The entrance to her home was made to look like a funeral parlor. Tablecloths were all black, with floral centerpieces of spider mums. The prime rib was tagged "side of salamander," and the tapioca pudding, "eye of newt."

Jones, who always enjoyed her spidery character on the show, frequently answered her telephone, "You rang?" She even appeared on "The Danny Kaye Show" dressed as Morticia. Flown from city to city on promotional tours for the show, she admitted being relieved when the rigors of travel ended and Astin could resume "chewing" on her arm.

Jones's second marriage was to conductor Herbert Greene in 1968; and she lived with him in Palm Springs in brief semiretirement. She later divorced Greene and married actor Peter Bailey-Britton, twenty years her junior. Jones continued regular television and film appearances after "The Addams Family." Her final series was the CBS daytime soap opera "Capitol," in which she starred as the manipulating power broker Myrna Clegg. She played this role for more than a year, until she was forced to leave the series due to illness.

Diagnosed with cancer, she had most of her stomach removed. For months she coped with the illness while receiving treatment. Sick, pale, and gaunt, she fell into a coma, her husband by her side. She died on

*Carolyn Jones as Marsha, Queen of Diamonds, leads Batman to the altar in an episode of the campy caped crusader's show. (Courtesy of 20th Century Fox Television)*

*Carolyn Jones continued to play Myrna Clegg in the CBS soap opera "Capitol" even though she knew she was dying of cancer. (Courtesy of Howard Frank Archives)*

August 3, 1983, at age fifty-four, a star of motion pictures and television.

## Additional Movie Appearances

*Invasion of the Body Snatchers; The Opposite Sex; Man in the Net; Last Train from Gun Hill; Baby Face Nelson; Saracen Blade; Little Ladies of the Night; Midnight Lace; Career; Ice Palace; How the West Was Won; Geraldine; Three Hours to Kill; Shield for Murder; Heaven with a Gun; The French Atlantic Affair; The Dream Merchants; Roots; Good Luck, Miss Wyckoff.*

## Additional Television Appearances

"Playhouse 90"; "Colgate Comedy Hour"; "Pepsi Cola Playhouse"; "Schlitz Playhouse of Stars"; "Four Star Playhouse"; "The Millionaire"; "Fireside Theatre"; "20th Century-Fox Hour"; "Jane Wyman Theatre"; "Wagon Train"; "David Niven Theatre"; "The Lloyd Bridges Show"; "Dr. Kildare"; "DuPont Show of the Month"; "Batman"; "Dragnet"; "Burke's Law"; "Rango"; "Love, American Style"; "Name of the Game"; "Mod Squad"; "Men from Shiloh"; "Ghost Story."

# "The Kid"

If Jackie Coogan is remembered for nothing else, his status in the motion picture industry will not be forgotten. He was the motion picture industry's first real child star, earning more than four million dollars before puberty. He was "the Kid."

Born in Los Angeles on October 26, 1914, baby John Leslie Coogan, a.k.a. "Jackie," debuted in films in a silent picture called *Skinner's Baby* in 1916, thrust into the business by his parents, who were show folks. His father, Jack Coogan, Sr., was a vaudeville hoofer, while his mother, the former Lillian Dolliver, had also been a dancer and comedian on stage.

His most famous movie role came in 1920, when Charlie Chaplin, already a star in silent films, saw little four-year-old Jackie in a stage show at the Los Angeles Orpheum Theater. As Chaplin wrote in his autobiography:

> I saw an eccentric dancer—nothing extra-ordinary, but at the finish of his act he brought on his little boy, an infant of four, to take a bow with him. After bowing with his father, he suddenly broke into a few amusing steps, then looked knowingly at the audience, waved to them and ran off. The audience went into an uproar, so that the child was made to come on again, this time doing quite a different dance. It could have been obnoxious in another child. But Jackie Coogan was charming and the audience thoroughly enjoyed it. Whatever he did, the little fellow had an engaging personality.

*Jackie Coogan became the movies first child star in 1921 when he and Char-
lie Chaplin premiered* **The Kid.** *(Personality Photos, Inc.)*

*Jackie Coogan being interviewed by PBS near the end of his life. He always carried some resentment about the financial woes surrounding his childhood earnings. (Courtesy of PBS)*

Chaplin was overwhelmed by what he had witnessed; he couldn't get the performance out of his mind. He went back to his studio and thought about a possible film vehicle to include this little waif. After hearing that Roscoe "Fatty" Arbuckle, the popular, chubby silent-film comedian, had signed Coogan to appear in a picture, Chaplin sank in defeat. But it was the senior Coogan whom Arbuckle had signed, and so the famous film tramp called the Coogans in for a meeting.

*The Kid,* released in early 1921, was the film Chaplin wrote and directed around Jackie: in it, a lovable tramp picks up an abandoned child, learns to love him, and gives him up for the child's own good. A climactic scene occurs when grubby workhouse officials drag Jackie away, heartbroken. Reportedly to induce sobbing from little Jackie, the elder Coogan told his son if he didn't cry, he really *would* be sent to a workhouse, which sent the little actor into a tearful fit. The scene went off without a hitch.

The film took a full year and three days to film, said Coogan: "It was an enormously long time to make a movie then, but [Chaplin] was writing the picture as we went along, and sometimes we would close down for ten days or two weeks while he got an idea. The picture was Chaplin's supreme effort, the test of whether he was a baggy-pants comic or a real fine actor. After the picture was made, his fame was greater than anybody's in Hollywood."

The fame was not cornered by Chaplin but, rather, shared by this curious little Coogan child whom the world came to love. Coogan and Chaplin were acclaimed by audiences and critics alike, and almost instantly their names became household words. Coogan, who stole the show in *The Kid* (Chaplin actually gave it away), became a major star, with an incredible merchandising campaign that followed, cleverly marketing this cute little kid's image on a clothing line, caps, Erector Set boxes, candy, dolls, coaster wagons, and much more. Jackie Coogan Productions was established with Coogan senior at the helm. This little boy wonder was displayed in films such as *Peck's Bad Boy* (1921), *Oliver Twist* (1921), and *My Boy* (1922). By 1923, Jackie was the number-one box-office attraction in America, ahead of Rudolph Valentino and Douglas Fairbanks.

More films followed for little Jackie (*Trouble, A Boy of Flanders, Daddy, Circus Days*), which further lined his parent's pockets.

In the summer of 1924, Jackie led a cross-country and trans-Atlantic "Children's Crusade" that raised thirty-five million dollars' worth of food and clothing to aid the children rendered homeless by the Turkish-Greek war of 1922. He rode a private train cross the country, greeting movie fans, smiling—always pushed by his parents to make this plea. In Greece, the government honored him with the Order of St. George and the Greek Orthodox Church presented him with the Cross of Justinian; in Rome, Pope Pius XI offered him the Papal Cross of the Order of Jerusalem.

For just signing with the newly consolidated MGM, Coogan received a bonus of $500,000, still a staggering amount. Little Jackie earned enough for his parents to invest in homes, automobiles, oil wells, and real estate. At MGM Coogan's company made the first million-dollar film, *Long Live the King*. In 1925, Jack Coogan, Sr., was responsible for intoducing starlet Lucille Le Sueur into motion pictures; she became better known as Joan Crawford.

Entering his teens, he made a few more films: *Old Clothes, Johnny Get Your Hair Cut, Tom Sawyer, Huckleberry Finn*. But as he matured, his appeal to audiences waned, and he gradually stopped making movies, paving the road for other children.

Writer Aljean Harmetz wrote in *The New York Times* in 1972, "What is difficult to comprehend now is the extent of Jackie Coogan's fame. He was the first child star. Of all the hundreds of child actors, all the dozens of child stars, who have followed him, only Shirley Temple came close to matching his effect on the national unconscious."

Though his childhood was far from normal, Coogan remembered it as being "the best." He was tutored privately until high school. Olympic swimming champ Duke Kahanamoku taught him to dive; when he was ten he played in golf exhibitions with Gene Sarazen; when other little baseball fans went to see their heroes play, Babe Ruth came to see *him*.

Just before his twenty-first birthday, his fairy tale turned into a nightmare. In a car collision, his father and three others were tragically killed; Jackie survived, badly bruised. When he came of age to collect literally millions of dollars earned as a youngster, his mother and Arthur Bernstein, the family business manager who later became his stepfather, refused to hand over what money was left (around $600,000 in cash and properties). At that time, under California law, the earnings of a minor became the property of the parents. "That would not have happened if my father [had been] alive," Coogan said years later. "I was very close to my father—very close. He wanted me to have the money."

What followed was a lawsuit against his mother and stepfather that dragged on for years, and was publicized in every medium across the world. Coogan's finances were plastered in every newspaper for the world to see. Finally, in August 1939, a settlement was made for $126,000, a mere crumb of the fortune amassed during his silent days. Although he never publicly blamed his mother for the dissipated fortune, Coogan held a personal tinge of anger for the rest of his life.

Because of the suit, the California State Legislature instituted what is formally titled the Child Actors' Bill commonly known as the Coogan Act, designed to prevent such abuses to children in show business. The bill mandates that at least 50 percent of a child actor's earnings be entered into a trust fund or some form of savings account for the child to collect when he comes of age. Although it protected hordes of child performers, stars such as Judy Garland, Edith Fellows, Freddie Bartholomew, and George "Spanky" McFarland of "Our Gang" fame were still to suffer at the hands of greedy rela-thieves.

By 1939, Jackie's two-year marriage to shapely starlet Betty Grable had crumbled, due to his financial ruin, among other reasons. He married three more times: Flower Parry in 1941, Ann McCormack in 1946 (both ended in divorce), and Dodie Lamphere—his last wife—in 1952. He had four children: Anthony (sometimes called Jackie, junior), Joan, Leslie, and Christopher.

After serving in World War II as a glider pilot, Jackie re-entered show business in stage acts and performed in legitimate theater productions. During television's infancy, he joined the cast of Irwin Allen's "Hollywood Merry-Go-Round," and later he was a regular on "Panto-mime Quiz." He received an Emmy nomination for his role as a comic cook in "Forbidden Area," the first "Playhouse 90" teleplay in 1956; and he starred in the sitcom "McKeever and the Colonel" just before landing the role of fat, bald Uncle Fester.

During the late fifties and into the early sixties, Coogan was arrested several times for possession of marijuana, highly publicized in newspapers. He was publicly linked with drugs and alcohol, but regained confidence emotionally, physically, and financially in the "Addams" decade. Undiagnosed for years, he suffered from sleep apnea and slept much of the time, plunging into a deep slumber at a moment's notice, though he was considered a consummate professional on the set and always was prepared for work. He strategically drove a motorcycle to work to keep him awake. "He kept three of 'em," says his daughter Leslie Coogan Franklin. "One to ride to work, the small scooter he used in the show—which eventually became mine—and the big one for the freeways and such."

Although Leslie maintains that she could write a *Fester Dearest* about the financial troubles and the emotional rues—*always* rooted in money—that upset her family, she contemplates channeling much of that material into a stand-up comedy routine that she is currently honing.

Leslie remembers one very poignant moment from her father's "Addams Family" days. "He had been doing the part for a while, I guess, and he came home crying—sober. He said, 'I used to be the most beautiful child in the world and now I'm a hideous monster.' That was heavy. Something just dawned on him one day. It hit him. He let go of it later, but it really had to do with his lost childhood. Later, he came to cope with the Fester character and loved doing the show. Then he cherished it."

After "Addams," Coogan continued to act in television and films and on stage. In 1972 he was reunited with eighty-two-year-old Charlie Chaplin when the legendary actor traveled from his home in Switzerland to the United States to receive an honorary Academy Award. Coogan and Chaplin chatted briefly in an emotional reunion that took place among crowds of movie fans and press. After his retirement in the late 1970s, Coogan lived in Palm Springs. He died from cardiac arrest on March 1, 1984, in Santa Monica Hospital. He was sixty-nine.

In a poignant moment during a 1972 interview, Jackie Coogan said: "What I'm proudest of is that no matter what I do now . . . I was the first. Nobody can ever take that away from me."

## Additional Movie Appearances

*Home on the Range; College Swing; Million Dollar Legs; Sky Patrol; The Actress; The Joker Is Wild; A Fine Madness; Rogues Gallery; The Shakiest Gun in the West; Cool Million; The Specialists; The Phantom of Hollywood; Sherlock Holmes in New York.*

## Additional TV Appearances

"Cowboy G-Men"; "Racket Squad"; "So This Is Hollywood"; "Matinee Theatre"; "Studio One"; "The Loretta Young Show"; "Peter Gunn"; "Lineup"; "The Adventures of Ozzie and Harriet"; "The Red Skelton Show"; "The Ann Sothern Show"; "Shirley Temple Theatre"; "The Tab Hunter Show"; "Guestward Ho"; "Klondike"; "The Outlaws"; "Perry Mason"; "The Andy Griffith Show"; "The Joey Bishop Show"; "Dick Powell's Zane Grey Theater"; "The Lucy Show"; "A Family

Affair"; "Here's Lucy"; "I Dream of Jeannie"; "The Wild, Wild West"; "The Outsider"; "Hawaii Five-O"; "Love American Style"; "Name of the Game"; "The Partridge Family"; "The Jimmy Stewart Show"; "McMillan and Wife"; "Adam-12"; "The Brady Bunch"; "Alias Smith and Jones"; "Cool Million"; "Emergency."

*Coogan and Cassidy toured the country. (Courtesy of the Academy of Motion Picture Arts & Sciences and the Jackie Coogan Estate)*

*Jackie Coogan with his young grandson, Keith, who has followed in the family profession (Leslie Coogan Franklin and the Jackie Coogan Estate)*

# Lurching Toward Success

 In 1964, towering Ted Cassidy suddenly uprooted himself and his family, quit his position as production director at WFAA, an ABC television affiliate in Dallas, Texas, and moved to Hollywood in hopes of work. During his assault on Tinseltown, he walked into producer David Levy's office with a brief background in radio and virtually no professional acting experience. Levy stretched his neck to make eye contact with the six-foot-nine, 250-pound titan, who uttered a deep "Hello." A little later, the actor walked out of Levy's office with the part of the hulking butler, Lurch.

Cassidy was born on July 31, 1932, in Pittsburgh, Pennsylvania, to parents no taller than five foot eight, and grew up in Philippi, West Virginia. Although his prowess in high school basketball and football might have suggested otherwise, he preferred acting to athletics, and his participation in high school plays planted a seed that would take root years later. He earned a degree in speech and drama from Stetson University in De Land, Florida, having previously attended Wesleyan College in West Virginia. After graduation, he had auditions and invitations to join Paul Whiteman as a singer and the Spike Jones group as a clowning warbler, but he rejected offers to pursue an acting career.

Cassidy married his college sweetheart, the former Margaret Helen Jesse, whom he called "Jess," and the couple had two children, Sean and Lynn Cameron, prior to his move to California. In the 1970s, he divorced Jess and lived with his girlfriend, Sandy.

The gentle giant struck others as a bit of an introvert. Co-star John Astin says, "Ted, like Lurch, was never completely happy with his lot. Ted expressed this. His height and look kept him from playing the roles

*Fearing severe typecasting, Ted Cassidy began to object to his role as Lurch the second season. (Personality Photos, Inc.)*

he wanted . . . sort of the giant who wanted to play Hamlet. Within the character of Lurch, I think he evoked all of that feeling. He was masterful in the character, and conveyed a beautiful world-weariness, and a deep sense of duty toward life—a sense of responsibility which Ted had."

The role of Lurch haunted Cassidy with a hovering gloom. Never really landing the roles he wanted, he continued to work from job to job, like most television actors. During and following his run in "The Addams Family," he guest-starred in episodes of "Laredo," "The Man from U.N.C.L.E.," "Mr. Terrific," "The Phyllis Diller Show," "The Monroes," "The Beverly Hillbillies," "I Dream of Jeannie," "Star Trek," "Lost in Space," and "The Girl from U.N.C.L.E."; and in 1968–69 he performed the role of Injun Joe in the short-lived NBC series "The New Adventures of Huckleberry Finn." Other television appearances included "Banacek," "The Six Million Dollar Man" (in which he played the hairy Bigfoot), and "The Bionic Woman," as well as one shot on "The Man from Atlantis." His movie appearances include *McKenna's Gold, Butch Cassidy and the Sundance Kid, The Last Remake*

*The Many Faces of Ted Cassidy. Top (from left): Injun Joe in "The New Adventures of Huckleberry Finn"; Lurch; Hachita in "McKenna's Gold"; and an evil genie in "Lost in Space." Bottom (from left): an Italian heavy in "The Girl from U.N.C.L.E."; an android in "Star Trek"; and Cassidy sans makeup. (Courtesy of Eddie Brandt's Saturday Matinee)*

*of Beau Geste, Benny & Barney, Las Vegas Undercover, Genesis II,* and *Planet Earth.*

Writer Joel Eisner talked to the actor in the late 1970s—a rare Cassidy interview—and asked him for his thoughts about playing Lurch.

"It was terrific until the second year," Cassidy said, "then I began to see that playing that guy, who really didn't do anything besides this shtick, was no fun. I began to react badly, not to the cast, the producer or director—because they were good folks—but to myself. I thought, 'I must get out of this show. This is terrible, I want nothing to do with this character, it's ruining me.' Everybody began to know me by the character's name instead of *my* name. I really began to panic, because if that keeps up, you never work again. . . . So I was really glad when 'The Addams Family' was cancelled.

"I have been trying to shake loose the butler image ever since. I can't tell you that I'm very fond of *anything* I've done, including—and especially—'The Addams Family.' "

Cassidy was concerned with another show-business association, this time, a mistaken one—with the even taller actor Richard Kiel, best known for his role as "Jaws" in the James Bond films *The Spy Who Loved Me* and *Moonraker*. "Now, there are quite a few people who believe that's me when they see him, which distresses me beyond telling," Cassidy said. "There was a point at which I was ready to get out of the business because of that—because he's not an actor. Not to me, he isn't. He does his best, but if that's acting, I'm a bricklayer. I can't really bear the residual effects of what he has done yet. I have to bear them, because apparently, half the world thinks that's me. . . . But for somebody to tell me, 'Oh, *The Spy Who Loved Me* was just terrific.' I don't think it was terrific. It was awful. That's the big dumb brute character again and I will *not* be known as that dumb brute."

A natural talent of another kind won Cassidy a host of other roles. With his rich, booming voice—which he greatly exaggerated for Lurch's grunts, groans, and gab—Cassidy turned to the voice-over field to pay bills. During the 1960s he provided the voice of the gentle superhero monster on the Saturday-morning "Frankenstein Jr. and the Impossibles" and other cartoon voices for "Birdman" and "The Fantastic Four" (as the rock-made Meteor Man). In the 1970s—despite his professed aversion to the character—he supplied the voice of Lurch in Hanna-Barbera's animated "Addams Family" series and also was heard as Godzilla in "The Godzilla Power Hour." For the first season of prime time's "The Incredible Hulk" (the live version starring Bill Bixby), Cassidy narrated and provided Lou Ferrigno's voice as the green giant.

Ted Cassidy died on January 16, 1979, at the early age of forty-six, of complications following open-heart surgery for a "nonmalignant tumor," according to *Variety*.

### Ted Cassidy Left in the Lurch?

When the actor died, his wife had him cremated and buried in the backyard. Not long after, widow Cassidy moved . . . and somewhere, in someone's backyard, is Lurch, resting peacefully under a shady tree.

# The Blossoming of Rock

 Yes, Blossom Rock was her real name. Known to many in Hollywood as actress Jeanette MacDonald's older sister, Blossom had a career in films and television of her own that rarely gets recounted.

She was born Blossom MacDonald on August 21, 1896, in Philadelphia. Although she began a career in show business before her sister did, touring in vaudeville circuits, it was Jeanette who gained a name. Blossom married Clarence W. Rock (who died in 1960) in 1926, and they toured together in an act called "Rock and Blossom."

In the late 1930s, a talent scout at MGM prodded Blossom to sign a contract, and she debuted in the Joan Crawford film *Mannequin* in 1937. On the advice of a numerologist (and for a five-dollar fee), she adopted the professional name Marie Blake, under which most of her work was credited. During the next few years, she made her mark in films playing Sally, the loquacious and inquisitive switchboard operator in the Dr. Kildare films, starting with *Young Dr. Kildare* in 1938.

Blake left MGM at the conclusion of the Kildare series and freelanced in motion pictures. She played Mrs. Quigg, one of the boarders in June Haver's *Love Nest* (1951), and continued her film career with bits in *The Brigand* (1952), *Small Town Girl* (1953), and *She-Devil* (1957). Fans of Paul Newman may remember her as his housekeeper in *From the Terrace* (1960). In all, she appeared in more than forty films during her career.

On television, she appeared on "The Phil Silvers Show" before landing the role that made her most famous—Grandmama, the shaggy elder witch on "The Addams Family."

*Grandmama relaxes on a bed of nails. This publicity photo, taken while film-ing the pilot presentation, illustrates the horrid makeup initially intended for Blossom Rock. (Wideworld Photo)*

With so many names to accommodate—Blossom MacDonald, Blossom Rock, Mrs. Clarence W. Rock, Marie Blake—her bank accounts kept getting mixed up, and so she settled on Blossom Rock as her legal and professional name in the 1960s.

Rock was an efficient performer, with a knack for comedy. She had champagne-colored hair and big, blue, kindly eyes and possessed a quiet personality off the set. She played Grandmama with a snappy delivery and a makeup imagery that closely matched Charles Addams's original cartoon character. Perhaps if she had added more depth or provided a wilder, more highly animated performance, she might have run with the role as Irene Ryan did as Granny on "The Beverly Hillbillies." But one outstanding, powerhouse Granny was all Filmways produced in the 1960s; and Blake, although she played the role adequately, got shoved under the carpet by critics.

Rock told a reporter for *TV Scout* in 1965 that Jeanette MacDonald

*Blossom Rock as Grandmama and unmasked (Personality Photos, Inc.)*

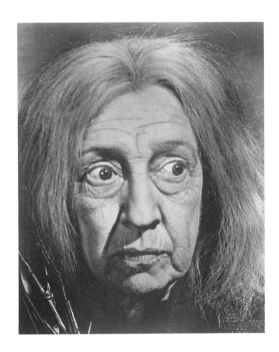

*Blossom Rock as Grand-mama (Personality Photos, Inc.)*

had gotten the "voice and beauty" of the family. "Actually I wasn't too bad looking until I broke my nose by running into a baby grand piano during my vaudeville days," said the comedienne. "After that, nothing could help. Not too many people recognize me as Granny on the show. I guess I would be insulted if they did. The only thing I regret is that I can't sing a note. On the show, we were to sing eight bars of 'Home Sweet Home' and they had to keep shooting it over and over because I was always off key."

John Astin, whose mother and Blossom became close friends, observed: "Blossom had a subtle and sophisticated sense of humor. While she played this haggish person, this was not Blossom at all. She was really an elegant and dignified personality. Gracious is a good word for her. Unpretentious, wise, and warm."

After the series, Blossom Rock quietly retired. In the early 1970s she suffered a massive stroke which greatly inhibited her speech, and prevented her from joining the rest of the "Addams" cast in the reunion movie of 1977; but she watched the ill-fated show on television from her residence at the Motion Picture Country Home. She died at age eighty-two on January 14, 1978. She had no close survivors.

## Additional Movie Appearances

*Love Finds Andy Hardy; Man-Proof; Rich Man, Poor Girl; Dramatic School; Day-Time Wife; Calling Dr. Kildare; I Take This Woman; The Women; Blind Alibi; The Secret of Dr. Kildare; Judge Hardy and Son; Dr. Kildare's Strange Case; A Child Is Born; Dr. Kildare's Crisis; Jennie; Dr. Kildare Goes Home; Dr. Kildare's Wedding Day; Remember the Day; I Married a Witch; South of Dixie; Gildersleeve's Ghost; Abbott and Costello in Hollywood; Christmas in Connecticut; Don't Trust Your Husband; The Snake Pit; Angel in Disguise; Alimony; Paid in Full; Human Jungle; Snow White and the Three Stooges.*

# Wednesday's Child

 Before she became Wednesday Addams, the pint-sized, pigtailed rascal who rarely smiled but took pride in the dolls she decapitated, little Lisa Loring was a top model from age three. She grew up in front of photographers, cameras, and directors on sets, with little remnants of an average childhood.

Lisa was born on February 16, 1958, on the Pacific island of Kwajalein, where her father was stationed in the Navy. Her parents divorced when she was two, and dainty Lisa auditioned for "The Addams Family" at the gentle age of six, when she couldn't even read. Out of nearly one hundred girls, David Levy, who created and cast the show, chose Lisa because she was a "precious, pretty girl" who readily repeated lines when fed them. Prior to the role of Wednesday, she had appeared on "The Art Linkletter Show" and in one episode of "Dr. Kildare."

Loring recalls little from her two years as one of the Family, because she was so young. "I don't have bright, vivid memories—just bits and pieces," she explains today. "I remember a strong family feeling. We were close, like a real family. I liked going to school with a tutor, but after a while I missed going to regular school. But I felt special, because there weren't as many kids on TV as opposed to today, where there are kids on every show."

Her television brother, Ken Weatherwax, attended school with her on the set, while guardians oversaw both children every hour of the working day. Did the youngsters get along? "Not at first," she reveals. "I think Kenny was jealous of me because I was like a little porcelain doll. John Astin, the director Sidney Lanfield, and the producer—all

*On the set of the original pilot presentation, which was shot at MGM using the existing set of the film* The Unsinkable Molly Brown *(Courtesy of Tod Machin)*

*A stunning Lisa Loring in recent years (Courtesy of Lisa Loring Siederman)*

adored me, because I was the youngest and I was a girl. I was treated special and he picked up on that. It made him feel left out, I think; but we didn't dislike each other. There was some friction. One time, I remember, the teacher had to put up a wooden partition between our two desks to keep us from picking on each other and throwing things."

On the set she was closest to Carolyn Jones and John Astin, surrogate parents of sorts. "John always said he was gonna adopt me away, because he only had sons at home," says Lisa. Her mother escorted her to the studio each day, but relinquished most of her maternal duties to her own mother, whom Lisa credits with raising her as a child. "My mother, who died when I was eighteen, was an alcoholic," says Lisa. "She was in and out of hospitals constantly. She had so many problems. So my grandmother took over, thank God."

Loring's childhood was short-lived. After her stint on TV she returned to public school and attempted a normal teen existence, which exploded in many directions. At age fifteen she was married. At age sixteen, she had her first child, baby Venessa, and came into her trust funds from "The Addams Family"—and sprouted many new fairweather friends. She was divorced at age seventeen. At eighteen, a stunningly gorgeous young woman, she rejected Hugh Hefner's request to pose for a *Playboy* centerfold.

Those years were difficult in some ways, she says. "When I was in public school, I realized people liked me because of who I was—or they hated me because of who I was," she says. "I went through quite a rough ordeal with other kids in that respect. I became bitter at a point.

"It wasn't until I was about sixteen or seventeen that I realized what 'The Addams Family' meant to a lot of people and that it had a cult following. A friend of mine took me to Alice Cooper's 'Welcome to My Nightmare' concert out here at the L.A. Forum in . . . I think it was 1974. We went backstage because my friend knew Alice. Press was there, celebrities were all over the place, Sal Mineo was there, actors, musicians. I was in awe. My friend whispered to Alice, 'Hey, you know that little chick over there—that's little Wednesday on 'The Addams Family.'

"Well, he *died!*" remembers Lisa, smiling. "He took a hold of my hand and started quoting lines to me that I didn't even remember. He kept saying, 'It's such a pleasure to meet you,' and on and on. My mouth was hanging open. I couldn't believe what I was hearing. I felt in awe to meet him. And a lot of other friends of mine in the music industry loved the show . . . guys from REO Speedwagon, the Eagles. When I got a little older, I thought, 'Hey, it's not as bad as I thought.' "

Loring made a television comeback when she lived in New York for four years playing Cricket Montgomery on CBS's soap opera "As the World Turns," beginning in 1980. She married a second time and had another little girl, Marianne, who wants to do commercials.

Today, Lisa lives in the Los Angeles area with her third ("and last!") husband, actor Paul Siederman, and her children. Siederman, a.k.a. "Jerry Butler," worked as an actor in the adult film industry for most of his adult life, starring in more than two hundred porn films—the cause of much speculation about their marriage. Lisa stands by her husband but cautiously explains: "I do not condone pornography or adult films, [though] I don't think they're harmful," she says. "But to each their own. I'm not involved in that, and neither is Paul anymore."

As Jerry Butler, Siederman wrote a shockingly blunt book in 1989 titled *Raw Talent*. Loring writes an epilogue for the tome:

> Our relationship was battered by many difficulties . . . [but] I don't care what small-minded people might think of my marriage. . . . The roughest part of the project was actually watching Paul's films. Knowing that people would be viewing the tapes made *me* feel naked, too. Anyone who saw us on the street or in the supermarket together could more or less picture what Paul did with me. But not really! No one can imagine the joy of our lovemaking. That intensity far surpasses anything you've seen on video or film.

She closes:

> I finally came to the conclusion that it doesn't really matter what anyone thinks about him or about us. The love, sensitivity, compassion, intelligence, and understanding of life that Paul has achieved is what is truly important and meaningful in a human being. And I have never found love so fully before.

After all has been said and done, "Jerry Butler," my Paulie, is a beautiful man and one hell of a person.

In an interview, Loring exudes confidence, a light sense of humor, and a practical view on many facets of her life. "I feel very lucky to have experienced what I have. Being on TV at an early age, it makes you grow up a lot faster. I'm that much more ahead of the game. It's made me who I am today, who I like very much."

Cosmetics Saleslady: Say, maybe you could help me make a sale . . . What kind of powder does your mommy use?

Wednesday: Baking powder.

Saleslady: I mean on her face.

Wednesday: Baking powder.

# Ken Weatherwax: TV's Pugsley

 Chubby little Kenny Weatherwax, the lovable Pugsley with slits for eyes and unkempt hair, was born into a legendary show-business family. His aunt is actress Ruby Keeler, who was married to entertainer Al Jolson during the 1930s. Another uncle was Rudd Weatherwax, the famous animal trainer and guardian of Lassie; Ken's half-brother, Joey (who went by the stage name Donald Keeler), co-starred for four years on TV's "Lassie," playing Sylvester "Porky" Brockway, Jeff's chubby sidekick.

Born on September 29, 1955, in Los Angeles, little Ken, like his older half-brother, entered the business at a tender age. His mother, Marge (sister to Ruby Keeler), introduced him to audiences as "Chester" in a series of highly popular Gleem toothpaste commercials in the early 1960s. ("We never used Gleem," Ken's mom confided.) The commercials, which co-starred Alice Pearce, the original Gladys Kravitz on "Bewitched," launched Ken into the public eye.

"He only wanted to do television because of his brother," says Marge Weatherwax, who raised him as a single parent. "Kenny got the role [of Pugsley] because of his exposure on the Gleem commercials. He tested with Carolyn Jones and got the part."

Ken's mother was permanently on the set with him when he filmed "The Addams Family," beginning when he was eight. She describes his years before the camera as pleasant experiences, although his interest in acting diminished quickly after the series. "He never enjoyed working," says Marge Weatherwax. "He just wasn't a professional child. He would have rather been off playing baseball or doing something else."

Carolyn Jones was quoted as saying, "Once Jackie [Coogan] noticed little Ken wasn't paying attention to cues. He poked him and said, 'Pay

*Courtesy of Milton T. Moore*

attention, kid. I did a law for you,' " referring to the famous child labor law the Coogan Act.

"Ken was a nice kid, but being a child actor can be a tough and unnatural life," says John Astin, whose son Sean, now a rising young film star, also began his career at an early age. "Imagine you are a thirteen-year-old kid, perhaps a bit overweight but otherwise normal. You have a life to live with your peers—and you go on a TV show as sort of an oddball character named Pugsley. He may have had some struggle there. Ken was a normal kid, and I'm not sure he wanted to be there. He was very dependable, congenial, and well mannered. I felt a great deal of affection for both kids on the show. Still do. I stay in touch with them."

Ken returned to public school after his "Addams" association and turned down offers from Walt Disney Studios to work in films. At age eighteen, he was given access to the funds set aside from his "Addams" earnings, and he splurged, as most any teen would. "He got his money then and that was bad," remembers his mother. "He just went to the bank, they said 'Here, sign this,' and he got the money. He loved it. He had a great time buying things. He got his own apartment and spent most all of it. Then reality hit him and he realized you gotta work for a living."

In 1977, Ken stepped in front of the camera, for nostalgia's sake, when he reunited with the cast for the TV movie *Halloween with the New Addams Family*. In 1988 he joined co-stars John Astin and Lisa Loring for an informal satellite interview from Los Angeles, broadcast to Australia, where an Addams renaissance was bubbling.

In more recent years, Ken Weatherwax returned to the business that nurtured him, this time behind the camera, working as a key grip and crew laborer on films and television shows ("The A-Team," "China Beach," "Full House"). Still overweight, six-foot-one Ken resembles actor-director Rob Reiner, and his face has changed little. He tends to regard his "Addams Family" years with indifference. He lives with his mom and aunt in Toluca Lake, California.

> Morticia: Life is not all lovely thorns and singing vultures, you
> know.

# The Long and the Short of Itt

*"xbsjywhspo ocmpszrgpuklhepfffff!"*
—Cousin Itt

 Maybe the most peculiar character on the show—if that's distinguishable—was a three-foot man made of hair. He sported dark sunglasses most of the time, and a little brown derby, and spoke in the vernacular of Martians. His name was Cousin Itt, and he became a cute, lovable member of the family. Naturally, the Addamses were the only people to understand his high-pitched gibberish, and occasionally they reciprocated the rattlings.

Cousin Itt fancied himself a magician, a comic, an opera singer, and a lover. When he wasn't hanging in the Addams chimney, he secluded himself in his miniature room equipped with matching miniature furnishings. He was the family mascot of sorts.

An Italian midget named Felix Silla, who stood three feet ten inches, enacted the diminutive and highly popular character, which even spawned a line of Cousin Itt dolls marketed during the show's run. He did not, however, supply Cousin Itt's voice. Silla donned the two-piece costume of hair (headdress and skirt) and pranced around the set for two years, avoiding lit matches.

"The costume wasn't heavy, but it did get hot sometimes," says Felix Silla. "In the beginning it was made of real hair. Then the costumers realized it was dangerous, because it would drag on the floor, and a lot of people in the studio and around the set would smoke a cigarette and drop it on the floor. So they went to a synthetic costume."

Under the locks of hair, Silla simply wore a black T-shirt and pants,

103

*Felix Silla in a studio portrait, 1960 (Courtesy of Felix Silla)*

*Gomez and Morticia crouch in Cousin Itt's studio apartment. (Courtesy of Felix Silla)*

with dark gloves in some episodes. Sight was difficult for Silla, beneath his coiffure of shedding shag; so when Cousin Itt slammed into a wall, he *really* slammed his head.

No stranger to performing stunts in films, Silla immigrated to America from Rome, Italy, when he was sixteen in hopes of finding work in show business. Means of employment were, and still are to a great extent, limited for individuals of his stature. He found work in the 1950s with the Ringling Brothers Circus in New York before venturing to Los Angeles to become the mascot at the Pacific Ocean Park amusement grounds. As "Commodore P.O.P." he greeted tourists, publicized the park, and toured the state. He appeared in the film *A Ticklish Affair* in 1963 prior to landing his first television role. Casting "The Addams Family," producers looked at Silla and said, "Itt had to be him."

The television show led to other work in the industry for Silla. Now in his mid-fifties, he was too young to perform in the most-watched film classic of all time, *The Wizard of Oz,* which was filmed just two years after he was born; although he's quizzed about his possible involvement almost daily. But he *was* introduced to his wife, Sue, by an original Munchkin from Oz, Margaret Williams Pellegrini. On Thanksgiving of 1961, Silla was passing through Phoenix en route to Los Angeles when

*Felix Silla peeks out from under the hair of Cousin Itt while Coogan appears to have just woken up. (Courtesy of Felix Silla)*

Pellegrini, a friend from years past, invited him to spend the holiday at her home with her family. Matchmaker Pellegrini introduced Silla to another little lady, and a long-distance romance budded during the next few years until Felix and Sue Williams were married in 1965. They have three children, Bonnie, Michael, and Diana, and reside in the Los Angeles area, where Felix remains active in the film and television industry.

After his "Addams" stint, Silla went on to perform under-costumed characters for Sid and Marty Krofft's Saturday-morning programs "Lidsville" and "H. R. Pufnstuf." He played Twiki, the shiny robot, on TV's "Buck Rogers in the 25th Century" and appeared in such films as *Little Cigars, The Black Bird,* and *Under the Rainbow.* Silla also performed stunts and doubled for children in films, working on such features as *The Russians Are Coming, The Russians Are Coming* and *Indiana Jones and the Temple of Doom.*

Today, Silla whisks around Los Angeles in his large, customized white Lincoln Mark VII with license plates that read TWIKI. Too bad they don't read ITT.

*Felix Silla in 1991 (Photograph by Stephen Cox)*

## ITT'S SHOWTIME!

Cousin Itt was introduced to America in the twentieth Addams episode, titled "Cousin Itt Visits the Family." As production personnel scurried to complete the show, Itt was not quite fully assembled—he was missing a voice—and the deadline was pressing on the postproduction engineers. Cousin Itt could be seen but not heard—until sound-effects engineer Tony Magro finally devised the exclusive formula that breathed audible life into the hairy little creature.

Magro remembers: "The producers were trying to think of some mechanical voice at the time. One idea was Itt would be a musician and he'd be riffin' all the time. I produced a chorus or so of just constant riffin'. That didn't sound right. Then I just started to talk fast as an idea. Then I talked naturally, but continuously, and speeded up the tape, like a mouse or rat might talk. I envisioned some guy that would be spitting words out because hair would be in his mouth. I fooled around with that idea, and the producers liked 'the fast rat.' "

As Magro describes it, he spit out gibberish in a sound studio, adding a *ppffffft* and a *thhhhttt* to some of the sentences in the dialogue, and accelerated the quarter-inch tape's speed. For nearly every episode, Magro analyzed the dialogue and recorded a new track for Itt's responses. (Late in the second season, a track of stock dialogue was produced for dubbing.) Magro strategically added intonation and emphasis on retorts, building a perfect sense of believeability for the character's dialogue, although these were some of the most outlandish, compulsive, and screwball verbalizations on television. Unlike the Chipmunks, Cousin Itt was never understood;

but his oration was hilarious nonetheless, and audiences went wild over his scenes.

Many myths have surfaced around the actual voice of Cousin Itt. Itt was not speech recorded and replayed backwards. There are no satanic messages underlying his harangues. And although producer Nat Perrin, in a *Variety* article, claimed that the vocals were his, the voice was provided exclusively by Magro. "In an interview, Nat Perrin once said he did the voice on the side because he was the producer. Filmways was afraid it might become an antiunion thing, since I was not a member of the actors' guild," Magro says of the company's tactic.

Until now, it has never been publicly revealed who provided the vocal characterizations for Cousin Itt. "I never got screen credit, but they paid me extra for it," says Magro, a sound-effects engineer since the 1950s. "Everyone in town knew it was me. Even my daughter still introduces me to her friends as Cousin Itt, and I have to go through the whole routine and give a few lines. It got so bad, my wife, Doris, used to call me to dinner using Itt's gibberish."

His daughter, Amanda, remains his biggest fan, says Magro, who admits she was an indirect inspiration for Itt's voice. "She was watching 'Captain Kangaroo' on television at the time," Magro says. "They had a rat on the show that they always tried to catch. It would come out and sneak back in. I got the impression that the sound they made for it was a phonograph played backwards or something. I toyed with that idea and took a hint from that. That produced Itt."

Magro, now fifty-seven, has been "handling film" since 1954, beginning at the film library at Fox. In the late fifties, he worked for the king of the B movies, Roger Corman, who pumped out a new movie every eight weeks. (Among his many films for Corman, Magro worked as the assistant film editor on the cult classic *Attack of the Crab Monsters.* Later he worked as sound-effects man on "Mr. Ed" and as sound-effects supervisor on "Switch" and "Magnum, P.I." His talents earned him an Emmy Award for sound effects for the TV film *The Executioner's Song,* and a second nomination for the TV version of *A Streetcar Named Desire,* starring Ann-Margret. Presently, he is associate producer of the highly acclaimed CBS show "Murder, She Wrote."

Oh, yes—if you're wondering, Itt's vocals remain in perfect tune. "bwpodziowlfpgtndkedoo!"

*Tony Magro, the voice of Cousin Itt, in a recent photo (Courtesy of Tony Magro)*

# The Addams Family Meet Frankenstein

 Curiously, there are many trivial-but-true ties between the Addams clan and Mary Shelley's famous monster, which actor Boris Karloff etched into the American imagination exactly sixty years ago.

Best known as Frankenstein's Monster, Karloff was the inspiration to cartoonist Charles Addams in creating the tall, hulking butler to the Addams Family. This quiet character became known to television audiences as Lurch. Karloff accepted this association and was even enamored of the thought that he'd be immortalized in an Addams cartoon. He enjoyed Addams's macabre style so much, he accepted the invitation to introduce one of the cartoonist's tomes. In his foreword to Addams's *Drawn and Quartered,* Karloff writes: "Playing a monster or two is a lot simpler for me than writing prefaces. . . . I hope I will not be accused of undue vanity if I publicly thank Mr. Addams for immortalizing me in the person of the witch's butler."

Think about it . . . the televersion of "The Addams Family" may owe more to Mr. Karloff than surface thought provokes. In the 1932 horror film *The Old Dark House,* Karloff gives a chilling performance as Morgan the butler; and other parallels between the film's and the TV show's settings and characters are uncanny. *The Old Dark House* may have been an unconscious pregnancy in the mind of the TV show's producer, David Levy.

It's too bad Karloff didn't make a visit or two to the Family on television—it would have been inspired. But Filmways Productions might not have preferred to cough up the funds Karloff was asking at the time. Lurch came face to monstrous face with Frankenstein, how-

*"Uuugggghhhhhhhh!"*
*(Courtesy of Howard Frank Archives)*

ever, when actor Ted Cassidy appeared in a television comedy sketch with the famed, sinister Karloff.

"Shindig," an ABC show with a teen rock theme, coupled guests Karloff and Cassidy on the October 30, 1965 episode. Karloff, disguised as a mad scientist, sang the popular "Monster Mash," with Cassidy, made up as Lurch, lying on a slab, emulating Frankenstein's Monster —the character Karloff created. (In the same episode, Cassidy debuted a new dance craze to his recently released single, "The Lurch.")

Interestingly enough, Karloff's co-star in Broadway's original production of *Arsenic and Old Lace* was Allyn Joslyn, who played Mortimer, the role Cary Grant rejuvenated in the filmed version. Joslyn had plenty of experience acting freaked out when he guest-starred on "The Addams Family" as Mr. Hilliard, the truant officer, in the premiere episode, and made his two subsequent appearances with the Family.

Directly after the "Addams" cancellation, that Frankenstein linkage crept into television again when Ted Cassidy supplied the voice for a campy cartoon version of the monster in "Frankenstein Jr. and the Impossibles." Cassidy's character was a fifty-foot, robotlike, caped superhero who answered the commands of his plucky friend Buzz Conroy, boy scientist. Buzz would speak the password "Allakazoom!" into his radar ring and the two would be off to destroy evildoers in Toontown. The Saturday-morning show, produced by Hanna-Barbera, ran two seasons beginning in 1966.

When TV's Stone Age family starred in the NBC special "The Flintstones Meet Rockula and Frankenstone" (1980), Cassidy was tapped yet again to supply the monster's penetrating voice. (He taped the lines many months before the special was completed and aired.) At this time, Cassidy was thankful to be working—monster or not—yet it's doubtful he was screaming "Yabba-dabba-do!" either.

*Frankenstein Jr. and the Impossibles (Courtesy of Hanna-Barbera Productions Inc.)*

# Wild Thing

*Do you remember the time Thing spilled salt and he almost went mad trying to find a shoulder to throw it over?*

*—MORTICIA ADDAMS*

 More than one dictionary describes the word "thing" as "a creature." Mmmm, you could say that. A lovable creature, though. This Thing is not to be confused with Thing 1 and Thing 2, the hellbent little characters who wreak havoc in a home in Dr. Seuss's *The Cat in the Hat.* And certainly our Thing did not co-star with Margaret Sheridan or Kurt Russell in either movie version of the suspense thriller *The Thing.*

So where did this Thing originate? Assumed by many to be the invention of executive producer David Levy, this creature's genesis actually long predates the Addamses' television debut, though possibly it was Levy who gave the character its fixed identity. The earliest fingerprints of the dexterous disembodied hand trace to Charles Addams's 1954 book of cartoons titled *Homebodies.* Addams's early exposure of Thing exhibited him protruding from an archaic Victrola, exchanging the records and lifting the needle.

Like Arnold the Pig on "Green Acres" or Carlton the doorman on "Rhoda," Thing on "The Addams Family" stole the show more than once and became a celebrated character of wonder. Everyone *wondered* why. One thing led to another (sorry!), and this helping hand became more than just a Thing of the past. Around 1970 he starred in his own series of commercials for Bell Telephone's Yellow Pages—"Let your fingers do the walking . . . ," which remains an ad slogan recognized by all. Needless to say, Thing is resting comfortably.

As a childhood companion of Gomez's, Thing was the Family's best friend. A most beloved character, which popped out of handsome, customized boxes in every room, this (for the lack of a better word) *thing* was a convenient little figure. Why didn't every home install a Thing? At the Addams home his duties included delivering mail (preceded by a loud *whoop! whoop!* sound effect), perusing the telephone book, taking shorthand, pouring tea, locking doors, fanning soup at the table, and even playing musical instruments. A versatile performer, this Thing did everything, and likably. He was a *he,* and mostly a righthanded he— although sleight-of-hand trickery can be caught in a few episodes where a lefty appears.

And maybe the most mysterious enigma enveloping the "Addams Family" production was the recurrently quizzed question "Who played Thing?" Simply put, Thing was the hand of actor Ted Cassidy, a.k.a. Lurch.

Giant Cassidy crouched under tables, scrunched behind scenery, and stretched around corners to give a hand and some personality to the lovable character, who appeared in almost every episode. Producers thought Cassidy's long, slender limb perfectly enacted Thing's personality, and Cassidy even signed a separate contract to roll up his sleeve and perform the handicraft. More than once Cassidy had to drive to the studio just to complete some shots that required Thing in the scene. He was not exclusive to the role, however. When the script required Lurch and Thing to appear in the same shot, assistant director Jack Voglin lent a hand and performed the role for the brief segment.

Until the mid-1970s, it remained a bona fide mystery who actually played the part. Publicists for Filmways and ABC attempted to suppress the inside information, creating an aura of mystique about Thing and the show.

Ted Cassidy explained to writer Joel Eisner for *Starlog* magazine: "I played Thing. I always have. In fact, I did Thing in the reunion [*Halloween with the New Addams Family*]. It was never publicized, although a few columnists were able to get it out there as show biz information, but no one seemed to really jump on it and be bowled over."

In "Portrait of Gomez,"
Thing is in a hollow tree
in the garden. He withdraws
his elbow is visible @ side of tree

### *Trivial Thing*

Episodes showing both Ted Cassidy and Thing in the same shot:

"Lurch's Little Helper"; "Addams Cum Laude"; "Morticia's Favorite Charity"; "Uncle Fester's Illness"; "Morticia, the Writer"; "Lurch and His Harpsicord"; "Halloween—Addams Style"; "Fester Goes on a Diet"; "Mother Lurch Visits the Addams Family."

**Artwork by Tod Machin**

# Les Mizzy Robbed?

 Vic Mizzy—his name is synonymous with television tunes, and the special brand of music that eerily erupts from his fingertips when he sits down to compose at an organ.

Mizzy is deeply distressed these days. A motion picture version of "The Addams Family" is in production, and to date, his talents have not been tapped to score the film. With a rascally smirk, Mizzy says he recently eyed actress Anjelica Huston, Morticia in the new film, sitting at the next table in a posh restaurant. He was tempted to secretly slip the nearby pianist fifty bucks to repeatedly play his "Addams Family" theme, just to irk the actress.

His ace is the original music for TV's "Addams Family," which remains recognizable the world over—and he has residuals to prove it. The familiar "ba-da-da-dum" from the refrain can be heard pepping up crowds at baseball games across the country. The special happy-but-weird sound unique to Mizzy's style brags an upbeat harpsichord saturated with an unusually heavy bass—both uncommon on television. In fact, "The Addams Family" was the first show to feature a harpsichord in its theme song.

Understandably, since it was one of the hallmarks of the TV show, Mizzy is disappointed that the new feature film may shun his theme. "The public's gonna expect the theme—I know it," states Mizzy flatly. He's not so disappointed that the producers of the "Green Acres" reunion TV movie in 1990 overlooked him. "Thank God!" he says. It flopped. The original "Green Acres" theme, hummed from Hooterville to Hollywood, is another of Mizzy's ingenious inventions. "I have what

*Vic Mizzy in the 1960s*
*(Courtesy of Vic Mizzy)*

they call the 'Green Acres' sound," he says. "I was one of the first to use a fuzz guitar on a television theme."

Both "Acres" and "Addams" have Mizzy to thank not only for the hit themes that became cornerstones of the shows, but for their lyrics, which helped shape pop-cultural Americana, and for his own brand of on-camera directorial technique for the opening segments of both programs. He remains one of the few composer-lyricists to have staged a show's opening sequence. The Addams Family snap their fingers to Mizzy's tune, while on another channel Oliver and Lisa Douglas enact a thirty-second "American Gothic" play telling the story of their move to the country ("Goodbye, city life!"). Outside of Mizzy, most composers stay in the recording studio—with the exception of Paul Henning, who wrote and produced the theme for "The Beverly Hillbillies" and Sherwood Schwartz who gave us "The Ballad of Gilligan's Island" and the "Brady Bunch" theme.

"I laid out that beginning and directed the whole main Addams title," Mizzy explains. "We brought a metronome on the set and had the cast snap their fingers to the beat. We shot it in about one take. I visualize a lot of things—my imagination runs beyond orchestrating and compos-

One of Vic Mizzy's biggest
hits during World War II
(Courtesy of Joe Wallison)

ing. It happened that way for several shows I scored."

Incessantly, it seems, this "Vic Mizzy" name appears on the television credits, and immediately two questions arise: Who *is* this Mizzy character? And is Vic Mizzy his real name?

The answers: Not many know. And yes.

Born in Brooklyn, New York, Victor Mizzy took organ lessons at age twelve. At age fourteen, he says, he wrote his first hit, "There's a Faraway Look in Your Eye," with Irving Taylor. At eighteen he enlisted in the Navy; and during World War II another of his songs, "My Dreams Are Getting Better All the Time," became a hit. Sung by Marion Hutton in the Abbott and Costello film *In Society,* it later was recorded by Louie Prima "and sold over two million copies," Mizzy says proudly. During and after the war, Mizzy continued to compose and write lyrics, turning out such pieces as "Pretty Kitty Blue Eyes," "Choo'n Gum," "No Bout Adoubt It," and "The Jones Boys." He's been married twice ("to the enemy," he says) and has two daughters, Patricia and Lynn. Today, he lives in an elegant house overlooking Stone Canyon Lake and maintains a studio with elaborate musical equipment. A collector of fine art, Mizzy decorates his home with paintings. On one wall hangs an original Matisse, while another room features two original Charles Addams works, all framed and tastefully displayed. He also owns race horses.

Of his compositions, his television tunes from the sixties linger most in popularity. Mizzy hit it big in television when he composed the "Addams Family" theme. It's been rumored that famed lyricist Johnny Mercer wrote the words, but ASCAP (the American Society of Composers, Authors and Publishers) lists Mizzy as the theme's lyricist.

"Originally, Filmways was going to use canned music," Mizzy recalls. "You know, music that was already around. David Levy, the creator of the show, knew themes were important. He was one of my best friends about that time. I don't know what inspired the words or music. You can't explain it. I am an impulsive composer—usually I go with my first thoughts." In this case, Mizzy was almost *forced* to go

*Musical wizard Vic Mizzy at his organ-synthesizer in 1991, playing his theme to* The Ghost and Mr. Chicken *(Photograph by Stephen Cox)*

## "THE ADDAMS FAMILY" THEME SONG

They're creepy and they're kooky,
Mysterious and spooky.
They're altogether ooky,
The Addams Family.

Their house is a museum,
When people come to see 'em.
They really are a scre-am,
The Addams Family.

Neat, sweet, petite

So get a witch's shawl on,
A broomstick you can crawl on.
We're gonna pay a call on
The Addams Family!

with his initial instincts, as deadlines did not permit noodlin' around with other possibilities.

Standing at a seatless piano, Mizzy played the theme song and snapped his fingers for Filmways executives and David Levy. The group instantly smiled, he says, and at that moment he knew the song would be a hit with audiences. The rickety old eighty-eight he plunked was said to be a "magical" or "lucky" old instrument played in many Deanna Durbin films and other hits. The chipped, warhorse piano had been shoved into a closet at the studio, forgotten until Mizzy pounded its keys one last time to test the lore.

Still, a deadline for the finished music nagged at Mizzy. "It was about two days before the pilot presentation was to wrap," he says. "I scored all the cues and laid down a basic track with the help of my music editor, Dave Kahn. He was a big help to me. To top it, Filmways didn't want to spend money for singers." What to do?

Mizzy and Kahn sang the theme song themselves on multiple tracks and looped Ted "Lurch" Cassidy saying "Neat, sweet, petite," between stanzas.

Following the huge success of the Addams melody, offers to score other TV shows and films were pressed at Mizzy. Of the films he chose to score, one in particular stands out as a whopping cult favorite among comedy film fans. Ever wonder who played the wild, eerie organ masterpiece in the Don Knotts creepy classic, *The Ghost and Mr. Chicken?* Mizzy. He not only composed and scored the film but was forced to perform the actual organ centerpiece of the film, because the orchestra's organist "froze."

---

### *More Mizzy Music*

**Television shows:** "Kentucky Jones"; "The Richard Boone Show"; "Shirley Temple's Storybook"; "Hank"; Klondike; "Temperatures Rising"; "The Pruitts of Southampton" (a.k.a. "The Phyllis Diller Show"); "Captain Nice"; "The Double Life of Henry Phyfe"; "The Don Rickles Show" (1968–69); "Quincy" (one season); "Delta House" (one season).

**Films and TV Movies:** *The Night Walker; Money to Burn; The Perils of Pauline; The Reluctant Astronaut; The Shakiest Gun in the West; How to Frame a Figg; The Love God; The Spirit Is Willing; A Very Special Favor; Terror on the 40th Floor; Don't Make Waves; Did You Hear the One About the Traveling Saleslady?; The Deadly Hunt; Hurricane; The Hound of the Baskervilles; Easy to Love; The Busy Body; Very Missing Persons.*

# Family Albums

 Composer Vic Mizzy produced an astounding stereo LP of original music from the show, released in 1965 by RCA. Rereleased in 1986 and still an incredible collection of contemporary sounds, this gem captured the true essence of the Family. In the liner notes, Charles Addams commented:

> From the moment I heard the first finger snap of the Main Theme, I felt that Vic Mizzy had captured the flavor of The Addams Family. All of the other themes contribute to the characterizations of the performers; for example, the aloof quality of Morticia, the engaging touch of Gomez, the somber but delicate air of Lurch. All of these melodic inventions are ingenious and all bear the trademark of exciting, fresh musical interpretations that mark Mr. Mizzy as the dynamic and original composer that he is.

In addition to Mizzy's album, a few other records are worth mentioning—and a few remain debatable.

Singer and songwriter Sonny Bono wrote and recorded a tune to the cue music associated with Thing. Bono expanded the Thing theme into a full instrumental song; it was an unauthorized version of Vic Mizzy's tune, however, and Mizzy's attorneys blocked the release with a court injunction against Bono in 1965. "He got pissed," said Bono recently. "It was called 'The Thing' and I did it with Charley and Brian, my two managers. We thought it was gonna be a hit. I liked the song— it was fun. We recorded it, but I don't think it got pressed up."

So Thing missed his chance for *Billboard*. Come to think of it,

Sonny and Cher might have made a perfect Gomez and Morticia! C'est la vie! Later on, Bono produced a retuned version of "The Addams Family" theme performed by a band calling itself Fiends. Originally released by Crescendo Records, the entry also appeared on an album titled *Horror Rock Classics* (Rhino Records). But if you still think your collection of Addams Family recordings is complete, consider these:

• "The Lurch," a 45 with talk-singing by Ted Cassidy, featuring a sixties female chorus behind him and the music of Gary Paxton. Flip side: another song by Cassidy, titled "Wesley." (Capitol 5503; released 1965.) "Uugghhhhhh!"

• John Astin warbled a 45 single also, titled "Querida Mia," during the height of the show's popularity. This is a rare find.

• Renditions of the show's main theme can be found on the albums *My First of 1965* by Lawrence Welk and his Orchestra (Dot Records); *Television's Greatest Hits* (TeeVee Toons); and *Elvira Presents Haunted Hits* (Rhino Records).

• Comedian Paul Lynde performed a hilarious Addams-esque comedy routine titled "The Family Just Across the Moat" on his *Paul Lynde: Just Released* album (Columbia Records). "Come give daddy a kick good-night. . . ."

• *Rerun Rock Presents Superstars Sing Television Themes* (Rhino Records, 1989) includes a rap version of "Gilligan's Island," a James Brown version of "The Brady Bunch," the theme for "Yogi Bear" à la the Cars, and "The Addams Family" sung by a Frank Sinatra sound-alike. "Dig! Who loves ya, Pugsley?" says Ol' Blue Eyes. It's pretty good!

Morticia: I know the effect you have on the opposite sex.

Gomez: Sometimes it frightens me.

Morticia: I live in constant fear that some woman will steal you away from me.

Gomez: Banish the fear, my Querida. You are the only cactus in the garden of my life.

# Addams Items

Of merchandise spawned by television series, "Addams Family" novelties are among the most pursued. The creepy, kooky toys, games, and collectibles are unearthed at swap shops and toy fairs around the country to this day. You may stumble on *neat* novelties, or a *sweet* treat, but not for a *petite* price. Among the items to be found:

- Uncle Fester's Mystery Light Bulb, by Poynter Products
- Addams Family Bubblegum Cards, by Donruss. Sixty-six cards per set, featuring photos from the television series. Originally sold for 5 cents a pack in 1964. A set of cards based on the Hanna-Barbera cartoon series was released in 1974 as a premium in bags of Wonder bread.
- "Addams Family" comic books, by Gold Key; only three issues produced, 1974–75; based on the Hanna-Barbera cartoons
- The Thing, by Poynter Products
- Addams Family Monster Eyes Flashlight, by Bantalite
- The Addams Family Game, by Milton Bradley; based on the Hanna-Barbera cartoon series
- Addams Family Mystery Jigsaw Puzzles, by Milton Bradley
- Morticia, Fester, and Lurch masquerade costumes, by Ben Cooper; include mask and pull-over costume
- Addams Family Card Game, by Milton Bradley
- Addams Family figurines, by Remco: five-inch dolls of Morticia, Fester, and Lurch
- Addams Family Cartoon Kit, by Colorforms

*The best thing about this Thing was the box. (Courtesy of Bob Morris)*

*These Family figurines are rare collectibles today. (Courtesy of Bob Morris)*

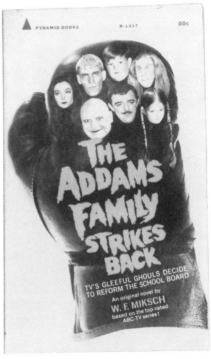

- Addams Family Coloring Book, by Saalfield
- Addams Family Hand Puppets, by Ideal: Fester, Gomez, and Morticia
- Addams Family children's wear, manufacturer unknown
- Addams Family Haunted House, by Aurora Plastics: an assembly kit of the TV house
- Addams Family Target Game, by Ideal
- The Addams Family Board Game, by Ideal
- Addams Family cloth dolls, based on the original Charles Addams cartoon characters
- Addams Family Collector's Plate, by Atlas China
- Charles Addams 1972 Mothers Day Collector's Plate, by Schmid Brothers; limited edition
- *The Addams Family* by Jack Sharkey: a paperback original novel based on the TV series (Pyramid Books, 1965)

THE ADDAMS FAMILY

*An Addams postcard merchandised in the 1980s (Courtesy of American Postcard Company)*

*An original Filmways publicity postcard mailed to fans who wrote to the cast of the show (Courtesy of Bob Morris)*

• *The Addams Family Strikes Back* by W. F. Miksch: a paperback original novel based on the TV series (Pyramid Books, 1965)

• Addams Family Lunchbox, metal, based on the Hanna-Barbera cartoon series

• Addams Family Postcards, by American Postcard; set of eight, with one in beautiful color

• "Fester's Quest" Nintendo software, by Sunsoft

• *Halloween with the Addams Family* (Goodtimes Home Video). This lame 1977 TV reunion movie in color, originally titled *Halloween With the* New *Addams Family,* is now offered on home video.

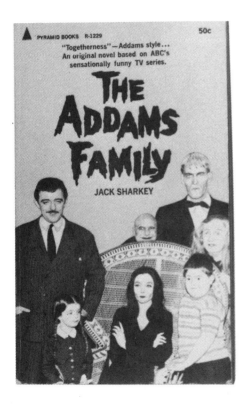

*The Family graced the cover of Mon-ster World magazine in 1966. The limited-run magazine is now a hot collectible. (Courtesy of Bob Morris)*

### *Family Heirlooms*

Some collectors, like Bob Morris, took their fascination with the horrific one step further. As a child growing up in the Midwest, Morris clung to Charles Addams cartoons from the moment he first picked up an Addams book at the local library. An amateur doodler himself, Morris wrote Charles Addams at *The New Yorker* and corresponded with the master of macabre.

"I've always liked dark humor," admits Morris, thirty-one, whose massive collection of Addams Family artifacts is probably one of the United States' leading accumulations. "Charles Addams is about as graphic in dark humor as you can get. He's the godfather. He's my Norman Rockwell, let's say. I think he and Hitchcock had a lot in common."

But Morris's eerie collection goes beyond one of the most complete aggregations of Addams Family toys. He boasts many original Ripley's Believe It or Not Museum artifacts (exhibits which commonly displayed authentic shrunken heads), rare authentic African and New Guinean native tribal artifacts, photographs of real African headhunters, and much more. Among his proudest acquisitions are personal items of the famed seventeenth-century witch hunter Matthew Hopkins. Skulls, Frankenstein lore, Dracula masks, and creepy horror knickknacks clutter the premises, while his wife's Liberace and Barbie doll collections pack another side of their house. Another lighthearted passion in the Morris household is fifties rock 'n' roll. Diversity knows no bounds with these cult collectors. Addams lives on.

*Addams aficionado Bob Morris with a few of his most prized collectibles.*

"FESTER"

**"Watch THE ADDAMS FAMILY on your local ABC station."**
©1964 Filmways TV Productions, Inc. ALL RIGHTS RESERVED.

Collect all 66 cards and place backs together to make a giant photo of THE ADDAMS FAMILY.

YES, THE REAL ESTATE IS GETTING CHEAPER.

**"Watch THE ADDAMS FAMILY on your local ABC station."**
©1964 Filmways TV Productions, Inc. ALL RIGHTS RESERVED.

Collect all 66 cards and place backs together to make a giant photo of THE ADDAMS FAMILY.

OF COURSE I PLAY THE PIANO!

**"Watch THE ADDAMS FAMILY on your local ABC station."**
©1964 Filmways TV Productions, Inc. ALL RIGHTS RESERVED.

Collect all 66 cards and place backs together to make a giant photo of THE ADDAMS FAMILY.

# A Festering Soar

 If you boarded an airplane and passed the cockpit only to notice Uncle Fester fidgeting in the pilot's seat preparing to guide the aircraft, you might immediately deplane.

In World War II, however, Lieutenant John L. Coogan accumulated more time night-gliding than anyone else—an excess of 8,500 flying hours. This was a record he was proud of, and Coogan spouted stories of the war when inquisitive fans or reporters questioned his 1940s Army Air Corps tour of duty.

Coogan enlisted in the army in 1941; three days after Pearl Harbor, he was sitting in a cockpit. He became a glider instructor and subsequently flew the California deserts at night for two years. Coogan was confident that the hundreds of hours of night flying saved his life when he volunteered for "hazardous duty" winging behind Japanese lines. Coogan was the lead pilot, the first man to land, in the air assault behind Japanese lines in Burma the night of March 5, 1944. Under the command of General Phil Cochran, he was a member of the First Air Commando Force led by Orde Wingate, the British brigadier. Eventually, Coogan was flying a succession of twenty-five to thirty missions a day.

Lieutenant Coogan was given an honorable discharge in 1944 and entered an assignment with Bond Drives. His decorations from the war included the Unit Citation Air Medal, OFC, and the Presidential Citation.

Coogan's experiences behind the controls of aircraft amid strategic strikes were so indelibly imprinted in his mind, he unconsciously manned the cockpit even while he dozed on a commercial plane. "We

133

flew together many times," remembers John Astin. "Jack had that ability to go to sleep anywhere and at any time, so on a flight he'd naturally go to sleep. As he slept, if you watched his feet and legs, he was automatically flying the plane. He brought it in for a landing! Jack was working the rudders—his feet were going back and forth. The plane would land and he'd settle down."

His ability to suddenly slumber combined with sinus complications he suffered made for interesting flights, Astin recalls. "There was an extraordinary echo in his snore, and it was extremely loud," says Astin, laughing. "Sometimes I'd have to give him a nudge because he was scaring the rest of the passengers. Of course with his head shaved and the two of us sitting there anyway, people looked a bit. But when Jack started that trumpet . . . I remember one person said, 'This is the first time I've been on a plane with *five* jets!' "

*Lt. John Coogan, July 1945, at George Field, Illinois (Army Air Corps photograph)*

# Double Duty

*The fair Ophelia!—Nymph, in thy orisons*
*Be all my sins remembered.*
                    —*William Shakespeare,*
                    Hamlet, *Act III, scene i*

As with the Doublemint Twins who chomped chewing gum in commercials, a favorite premise in sitcoms was the hybrid hijinks of look-alike relations. A double whammy—you know, two for the price of one. In the case of "The Addams Family," you'll recall that actress Carolyn Jones played both Morticia *and* her homely blond flower-child sister, Ophelia, whose never-ending quest for love often brought her to the Addams home for a good cry.

Her Shakespearean namesake was the love of Hamlet, described as a "fragile and passive creature . . . overwhelmed by the tragic events around her." Their personas were interchangeable. But TV's Ophelia had an advantage over *Hamlet*'s: she was an expert judo practitioner, flipping Gomez in every room—whenever she felt the urge. Gomez felt thine agony.

"The Addams Family" was not the first sitcom to use this device. Usually, both characters, portrayed by one actor, are not clones, but obnoxious opposites in personality. Thus, the actors who assumed the double duty felt satisfaction in this departure from the weekly character they played.

Here follows a listing of sitcom's Top 10 Double Images. Remember thy characters?

*Carolyn Jones's dual roles: Morticia and Ophelia (Courtesy of Howard Frank Archives)*

1. Morticia Frump Addams and her single sister, Ophelia, in "The Addams Family," both played by Carolyn Jones.
2. Patty Lane and her identical cousin, Cathy Lane, on "The Patty Duke Show," both played by Oscar-winning actress Patty Duke.
3. Samantha Stephens and her nearly identical cousin, Serena, on TV's "Bewitched," played by Elizabeth Montgomery.
4. Jeannie and her sister, Jeannie II, on "I Dream of Jeannie"; both were Barbara Eden. (Bonus: The master of Jeannie II, Habib, was played by Ted "Lurch" Cassidy.)
5. Jethro Bodine and his strapping sister, Jethrine, on "The Beverly Hillbillies." They were actor Max Baer, Jr., in and out of drag; Jethrine's voice was provided by Linda Kaye Henning.
6. Bob Collins and his aged father, Josh Collins, on "Love That Bob," both portrayed by Bob Cummings.
7. "Alice" Nelson, the maid, and her identical cousin, Emma, an ex-WAC, on "The Brady Bunch," both were Emmy-winning actress Ann B. Davis.
8. Herman Munster and his primitive cousin Johann—another prefabricated Frankenstein's Monster—on "The Munsters"; the pair were performed by Fred Gwynne.
9. Steve Douglas and his Scottish kinsman Lord Fergus McBain Douglas on "My Three Sons," both played by Fred MacMurray; the voice of the Scotsman was provided by Alan Caillou.
10. Captain Merrill Stubing and his menacing brother, Marshall, on "The Love Boat," both played by Gavin MacLeod —the latter with toupee, the former without.

Honorable Mentions: Although scripted as nonrelations, a whopping three dual roles were enacted in separate episodes of "Gilligan's Island." Remember? Identical imposters of Thurston Howell III, Gilligan, and Ginger Grant all visited the island, subjecting double duty to actors Jim Backus, Bob Denver, and Tina Louise, respectively. Actress Barbara Eden also portrayed a wild variety of relations, including her own mother, in "I Dream of Jeannie."

# The Addams Family Tree

*Some of the finest men in the Addams family have been shaped by childhood traumas!*

*—Gomez Addams*

Any random visit with the Family might introduce you to the wackiest chronicle of relatives ever mentioned on television. The Addams kin was a Wacks Museum of creatures with a long, dark history buried beneath them . . . nearby, of course.

At one point, a genealogist was engaged by Gomez to trace the roots of the family. Initially, the researcher assumed they might be related to the New England Adamses, John and John Quincy. "That's been a great source of embarrassment for us," recoils Morticia with disgust. "It's Addams with two *d*'s," Gomez is swift to clarify.

What follows is a table of Addams ancestry. I've attempted to index a tour of the Addams bloodline, gathered from the memorable anecdotes revealed in the episodes. Expect a little genealogical disorder and illogic on this family tree. This old oak has a few bent branches and broken limbs.

Remember these kinfolk?

*Admiral Addams: they hanged him 200 years ago.*

*Aunt Anemia:* She had a beard, "but never a mustache!"

*Aunt Blemish:* Morticia mistook her for the old Addams barn in a family photograph.

*Aunt Drip:* Married to Uncle Droop (he had bulging eyes). Their portraits hang in the playroom.

*Abigail Adams and the rest of those Boston two-d'd Adams's are related*

*Aunt Phobia:* Gomez once hid a hornet's nest in her sleeping bag. *Aunt Trivia was not a music lover; she just liked to go around kissing harpsichords.*

*Aunt Vendetta:* No description of her exists.

*Black Bart Addams* and *Bloody Addams:* A professional genealogist traced the family to these characters. Unfortunately, no descriptions of them are available.

*Brother Clump:* Fester's "dearly departed" brother.

*Commodore Addams:* Spoken to the ol' commodore as he led his men off a sinking ship: "It's wonderful the way you just leap in, take charge, and lead the way."

*Cousin Bleak:* Boll weevils infested his hair. What a mess!

*Cousin Blob:* He was "deathly afraid of ghosts—now he's one himself," said Gomez. The family hears him on dark, stormy nights.

*Cousin Cackle:* He used to reside in the Addams attic before moving to a cave, where he's lived for more than thirty years. This Moses look-alike, who screams with an unflagging, wild, maniacal laugh, appears in one episode, "Halloween—Addams Style."

*Cousin Caliban:* He had two heads.

*Cousin Clot:* He was sentenced to the electric chair. (Gomez: "I'll never forget the day the judge imposed sentence . . . Clotty stood there, head high, shoulders back, said, 'It's a bum rap.' " Morticia: "Addams to the end!")

*Cousin Creep:* Pugsley accidentally zapped him with a disintegrator ray gun. Fester remembers, "There he was, giggling and laughing. Suddenly, there he wasn't—still giggling and laughing. It was kind of eerie."

*Cousin Crimp:* This two-headed individual (one male, one female) was "such fun on double dates," according to Morticia. Gomez said Crimp was "mighty handy when we needed a third or fourth for bridge, too." Crimp used to love to play the harpsichord and passed the family musical heirloom down through generations; he used to play four-handed compositions on it—all by himself. Crimp had one glass eye. *Also, could use a 10+ /to shawl*

*Cousin Cringe:* The family sealed a hacksaw in a pie and passed it to Cringe in jail. He ate the hacksaw, too. "In fact, he developed a taste for them," Morticia remembers.

*Cousin Curdle* had a head turned around backwards.

*Cousin Droop* dropped a mirror for luck.

*Cousin Ferook* was nearly consumed by a swordfish. The remains of both Ferook and the fish are mounted on the wall. *

*Cousin Goliba was a bad bathing suit)*

*Cousin Goop:* Gomez said, "Now there was a fellow who really knew how to look for a job. Never found one."

*Great,, Great-Aunt Singe (she was burned at Salem)*

*Cousin Gripe* attained a mate through a marriage brokerage called Hasty Marriage.

*Cousin Grisly:* A portrait of Grisly facing a firing squad hangs in the Addams hallway.

*Cousin Grope* had three ears.

*Cousin Imar* had three arms. Morticia knitted a sweater for him.

*Cousin Nanook — see p. 31*  *Cousin Manuela was a pyromaniac ("You Castilians are so fiery!")*

*Cousin Plato* had two heads. The left head was size 6, and the right, size 8¾. Morticia knitted him a custom ski cap.

*Cousin Slimey* had two heads.

*Cousin Slosh* went down the city sewer in a "fit of pique" and completely disowned the family. "Made a whole new life for himself," said Gomez.

*a/k/a* *☆ Cousin Squid (in Festus' toupee)*

*Cousin Turncoat:* No description is available.

*Cousin Vague:* "He's about as abstract as you can get," says Gomez.

*Ol' Ebenezer Addams* led the early settlers across the Great Plains and sold the first guns to the Indians.

*Edwin Booth Addams:* No description is available.

*General Ulysses S. Addams:* At Vicksburg he surrendered— but "not until they caught up with him," Gomez adds.

*Grandfather Malaplop:* Fester molded a ceramic urn for him. ("Oh, how thoughtful!" Gomez said. "He *is* getting on.")

*Grandma Squint* reportedly makes strange sounds from the attic.

*Grandpa Squint:* Abraham Lincoln begged Squint for his political support, but, alas, the man who got it was Stephen Douglas. In the political realm, Gomez notes, rather than run for office, "We Addamses prefer to think of ourselves as king-makers."

*Grandpa Droop* gave Morticia stock certificates for her twelfth birthday.

*Grandpa Slurp,* a "handsome devil," had a bucktooth and a receding chin.   *Grandpa Squid — wrote medical book*

*Granduncle Grisly* was a traitor—but he only did it for the money.

*Great-Aunt Deliria* was engaged to a chimpanzee.

*Great-Grandfather Blob* pried a sacred ruby from the hand— er, *head*—of a Hindu (it was causing a terrible headache). The relieved Hindu presented the gem to Blob, and it became a family heirloom. Fester sold it off cheap when he needed money.

*Great-Grandfather Pegleg Addams:* The last of the adventurous Addamses, he wore a pegleg just for appearances, and was wanted by fifteen countries for piracy. He was buried at sea with full military honors: blindfolded, handcuffed, and dropped off a plank.

Morticia knits a three-armed
sweater for Cousin Imar.
(Courtesy of Milton Moore)

*Great-Great-Grandmother Slice:* A distant grand to Grandmama, she sharpened guillotines. "The belle of the French Revolution," Morticia brags.

*Great-Great-Great-Aunt Singe:* She was burned at Salem. (The family keeps her ashes in an egg-shaped urn.) Morticia organizes a séance in an attempt to reach Aunt Singe, and proclaims this incantation:

> Fire of Salem, ol' flame of Satan—
> Come in Aunt Singe, we're all awaitin'.

*Mamoud Khali Pasha Addams:* In A.D. 270 he used a torch to set fire to the library at Alexandria, Egypt. "The firebug of the Bosporus," says Gomez.

*Old Senator Addams:* "So wise and understanding," they said about him just before they impeached him, Gomez reveals.

*Sir Newton Addams* was a scientist who set his house on fire during an experiment—the high point of his career.

*Uncle Blight:* nicknamed "Ol' Kiss-of-Death Blight" (Gomez never knew why), Blight heavily backed the presidential campaigns of such washouts as Wendell Willkie, Alf Landon, and Adlai Stevenson.

*Uncle Tic:* Married to Aunt Phobia, "he had two left feet, she had two right ones. It was a mere physical attraction," Fester explains.

*Carolyn Jones with her alter egos Morticia and Ophelia (Courtesy of Howard Frank Archives)*

# Gruesome Twosome

*Exactly why two networks should come up with
two shows in the same year on exactly the same
subject and with two families which, if you asp us,
are dead wringers for each other, would take, we
suspect, grave explanation.*
                    —TV Guide, *November 1964*

 During the Golden Age of Sitcoms (the sixties, of course!), cowboys and castaways, surgeons and spies, hillbillies and genies all had their day. In 1964, it was the Year of the Ghouls when both "The Addams Family" and "The Munsters" burst upon television like a spray of lightning over the Bates Motel. Ironically, both shows premiered—and later got axed—in the same weeks. The shows were constantly compared, and a friendly rivalry of sorts developed between them. Cleveland Amory wrote in *TV Guide:*

> We have an uneasy feeling that once ABC had gotten hold of the idea . . . someone left the morgue unlocked one night and lo and behold, when the shrouds lifted there was not one, but two new chillbilly shows . . . On the other hand, for all we know, CBS had the idea all by itself and the whole thing was just a ghastly coincidence—part, if you will, of America's vultural explosion.
>
> Poisonally, however . . . the choice is easy. Of the two corpus delicti, ABC's "The Addams Family" is far and away the most delectable.

*The Munsters, TV's First Family of Fright (Courtesy of Al Lewis)*

And one comedy writer maintained that the Addams Family "had a lot more class than [their] neighbors . . . the Munsters, who always came off looking like poor relations."

If select sides you must, however, the position to choose might be the neutral standpoint, emphasizing that the shows *shouldn't* be compared at all. If you ponder, you'll realize the Addams clan originally conceptualized by the cartoons were malevolent creatures. Then they became television's first countercultural role models—and truly weird ones—"in an age when non-conformity was beginning to be regarded as an asset, not a liability," one critic alluded. "TV's proto-punks."

The Munsters were a hearse of another color. Patterned on a stable of Universal Studios monsters, this fun-loving "average" family was created by Bob Mosher and Joe Connelly, the folks who gave us "Leave It to Beaver." The Munsters, TV's First Family of Fright, suggested macabre humor like the Addamses but resided in a cobwebby, unpleasant dungeon of a house. The Munsters were humorously grotesque and held back on the whimsical, the oddball and the outlandish—much different from their "competitor."

But the creator of television's "Addams Family," David Levy, concedes that if it weren't for "The Munsters," there might not have been an "Addams Family": "I give them that due." As *New York World-Telegram* columnist Al Salerno reported, Edgar J. Scherick, vice-president of programming at ABC in 1964, announced plans for "The Addams Family" days after CBS's declaration of "The Munsters."

"Addams" producer Nat Perrin recalled: "Curiously enough, David Levy had taken this show to the networks some time before and was shrugged off. It was only because of a show which I couldn't stand, really—'The Munsters'—an asinine show. They got on, and David went back to the network and said, 'A fourth-rate imitation of 'The Addams Family' gets on, and I bring you the *real* thing . . . the *real* characters!' He sold it."

John Astin recalls the National Association of Broadcasters convention of 1964 in Chicago. Pilot presentations of both "The Munsters" and "The Addams Family" were premiered to network executives, critics, and audiences. "The 'Addams' presentation was extremely successful in Chicago," Astin says. "I heard 'The Munsters' was not well received. In fact, they recast. The actress they had for Lily, Joan Marshall, looked more like the cartoon of Morticia than Carolyn Jones. Carolyn had a slightly roundish face, and Joan had a long, slender face that closely resembled the Addams drawings."

Ultimately signed for the ensemble were Fred Gwynne as the lovable, bumbling Herman Munster and former movie queen Yvonne De Carlo as his headstrong wife, Lily. Al Lewis was a perfect choice for cantankerous Grandpa, Lily's father. Butch Patrick was little Eddie Munster, the boy who pioneered Spock ears two years before Spock. And Beverly Owen was cast as poor cousin Marilyn, the black sheep of the family—i.e., the only normal-looking one in the bunch.

Their house at 1313 Mockingbird Lane, an extraordinary piece of construction, was an exquisitely decorated spooky mansion kin to the Norman Bates residence in *Psycho,* ridden with bare trees, tumbleweeds, and broken shingles. Clouds hung over it continuously, and on a good night an occasional bolt of lightning would blast the roof. Inside, the home was dominated by a huge staircase. In a living room full of

*Yvonne De Carlo as Lily, the Munster matriarch (Courtesy of Yvonne De Carlo)*

*Al Lewis, everybody's favorite "Grampa" (Courtesy of Al Lewis)*

Gruesome Twosome   147

dusty antiques, a peculiar cuckoo clock sat in one corner: when it struck, a raven peeked out to yell "Nevermore!" Grandpa mixed potions in a fully equipped dungeon while Eddie played with bats and the family pet, Spot, a fire-breathing dinosaur that lived under the staircase.

Here are a few Munster morsels from the show:

• With lunchbox in hand, Herman Munster arrived to work each day at the Gateman, Goodbury & Graves funeral parlor. He started out as a humble "nail boy," but a shroud of mystery surrounded his actual duties. He was quoted as saying: "Sorry I'm late, but before I left I had to lay out some work for tomorrow," and "Starting Monday, I'll be driving the hearse—or as they say in the trade, the go-go wagon."

• Two popular mainstays of the sixties' kinky-car craze were the wacky Munstermobiles: the Munster Koach and the Dragula. Created by the "King of Kustomizers," George Barris, who also gave us the Batmobile and the Monkeemobile, the Munster motors enjoyed vehicular celebrity and were offered by a.m.t. as model kits.

• With his wild, graying sideburns and an acute widow's peak, old Grandpa fancied himself a mighty wizard. Items in his magical chest included a Mother's Day card from Lizzie Borden, a rabbit's foot carried by General Custer, and a compass off the *Titanic*. Always experimenting with potions in his lab, he invented a pill that turns water into gasoline, an alarm-clock pill which wakes you at a desired time, and athlete's foot—his brain child. Spells cast: "Don't let time or space detain ya—off you go to Transylvania!" and "Abracadabra and asee dosee, allakazam and Bela Lugosi!"

• Lily Munster, the devoted wife and mother, was constantly in the kitchen brewing sumptuous meals from recipes handed down through generations: cream of vulture soup, curried lizard casserole, rolled hyena-foot roast, or dodo bird roast.

• Marilyn Munster, the man-hunting cousin who never quite fit in, was portrayed by two actresses during the series. For the first thirteen episodes, New York actress Beverly Owen was the blond Marilyn Monroe–Sandra Dee character. Owen never wanted to do the series but was wrangled into it; she balked so much, producers released her from her contract. Pat Priest, daughter of former United States Treasurer Ivy Baker Priest (her name is featured on some currency), assumed the role and finished the series.

The makeup and the other technical aspects of the series were exceptional. Universal Studios devoted quite a monstrous group of experienced personnel—many of whom had worked in Universal's original horror flicks—and a whopping sum for production costs. The special effects were perfect, and the cast's extensive makeup could consume up to two hours each day to prepare. While the rigors of such a schedule made Fred Gwynne grow to despise the character that boosted him to fame, his friend Al Lewis took a shining to his "Grampa" character, publicizing the ol' gentleman in a variety of ways, including his own Italian restaurant of the same name in New York.

"The Munsters" completed a total of seventy episodes at Universal, including a full-length color motion picture released in 1966, titled *Munster, Go Home!* The show spawned a cartoon pilot, a comic-book series, a gallery of Munster merchandise, and, in 1981, an ill-fated TV reunion flick (aren't most TV reunions ill-fated?) titled *The Munsters' Revenge*. In the late 1980s Universal dredged the monsters from the dead for a new, cheaply rehashed, horror-ble TV show, "The Munsters Today." Starring John Schuck and Lee Meriwether as Herman and Lily, this videotaped monstrosity is noxious beyond description—so awful, in fact, it deserves no further words. Needless to say, fans were driven back by fiery torches to syndicated reruns of the original show.

In an October 1964 *Newsweek* letter to the editor, a Mrs. John L. McCarty of Ashland, Kentucky, made the plea: "May I present my first candidates for removal from this season's television schedules—'The Addams Family' (ABC) and 'The Munsters' (CBS). What's so funny about these overplayed comic-horror stories? Here's my vote against sick, pseudo-comedy." Thus proving that yet a third opinion exists on the subject of the two shows: yes, there were viewers who despised *both*. In 1966 McCarty got her wish. Did she know someone at the networks?

But monsters and ghouls never die . . . and the legacies of these two shows live, to be immortalized in books such as this.

### *The Lessons of Two Evils*

Remarkably, there are as many coincidences and similarities between the Addams Family and the Munsters as between Lincoln and Kennedy. Did you know . . .

• Both series premiered and received network pink slips during the same weeks.

• Although both were successful in the ratings, neither was nominated for an Emmy.

• Sexual creatures were these: both series got away with murder from network censors. Gomez and Morticia took liberal steps with their kissing and lovemaking innuendos, while Herman and Lily have the distinction of being the first TV sitcom couple to be shown together in the same bed—'tis true! (Many assume that Mike and Carol Brady were the bedroom breakers.)

• While his old man was starring as Uncle Fester, Anthony Coogan, a.k.a. Jackie Jr., guest-starred on an episode of "The Munsters" ("A Man for Marilyn").

• Butch Patrick, who played Eddie Munster, later played Pugsley Addams in a CBS-TV special in 1978, "The Addams Family Funhouse." The show starred Jack Riley as Gomez, Liz Torres as Morticia, Stubby Kaye as Uncle Fester, and Pat McCormick as Lurch.

• Composer Vic Mizzy, who wrote the "Addams" theme song, later scored the Munsters' 1981 NBC-TV reunion movie, *The Munsters' Revenge.*

• Both shows played host to Don Rickles, Richard Deacon, Lee Bergere, Bella Bruck, Elvia Allman, Jimmy Cross, and Olan Soulé, among other actors.

• Grandpa Munster and Gomez Addams both puffed diligently on cigars.

• Funny, but more than just a few "Addams" and

"Munsters" episodes had hauntingly similar plots. Both families went on a treasure hunt, discovering a chest of fortune on their own property. The children of both families ran away. Both families filmed spacemen episodes (common in the 1960s), while each show devoted a storyline to the parents' mistaken assumption that their little boy had been transformed into a chimp. Beatniks discovered both families. Each show presented a leading character going on a hopeless diet. Both families built robots. Arguments erupted in each brood and someone painted a white line to separate the house. Family pets were missing in both shows (with the Addamses, it was Thing), just as both Herman and Gomez suffered from massive amnesia. And finally, both cantankerous characters—Grandpa and Fester—ran newspaper ads advertising for a mate.

Hmmmmmmm.

Gomez: Fester, this may be a trespasser and a saboteur, but he is our guest.

# The Addams Bomb

*Alas, "The Addams Family" should have been left to rest in peace, for even with four of its original stars, this offering, in entirely inappropriate color, was a ponderous and stupid thing. It kicked off badly with a heavy-handed re-arrangement of the jaunty theme and went downhill fast.*
—FRANK GAUNTLETT, **Australian Daily Mirror**

 One of the earliest sitcom refluxes—even before Gilligan was finally rescued—was an "Addams Family" reunion, in color, with the original stars from the series. *Halloween with the New Addams Family* could have been a wonderful trip down memory lane for fans of the sixties cult hit. When the project began, it seemed to have potential . . . until it was written, and acted, and scored, and produced, and finally aired as NBC-TV's "Big Event" on Sunday, October 30, 1977. It *was* a "big event"—but so were similar calamities like the Edsel and the *Titanic*.

Many elements from the original show returned for this made-for-TV movie, which allowed audiences to once again pay a visit to the Addams house. All of the original cast except Blossom Rock, who was too ill to work, reunited, along with frequent guest stars Parley Baer and Vito Scotti. Original producer David Levy spearheaded the project once again, Vic Mizzy scored the music, and the costumes and makeup remained the same. But many elements did *not* reappear—most notably the laughs.

As an experiment, the entire production was shot on videotape on location in a house in Los Angeles which had previously been used for the film *Ben*. The mansion did not directly resemble the original, though the outside might have passed. But the inside bore a poor resemblance to the wacky original—it was cheaply decorated and poorly planned—and the lighting, difficult under these conditions, provided no imagination. The use of color with the Addamses consciously disturbed the image, and the laugh track sounded like it belonged on TV's "Diff'rent Strokes." The script lacked the character interplay of the original show. Too many non-Addamses and foreign elements were introduced.

The cast's performances were mostly hearty and similar to their sixties work, although Jackie Coogan, who was recuperating from a mild stroke, had aged drastically and sounded gruff and tired—he appeared to forget how to perform the ol' Fester. Felix Silla once again wore mounds of light brown hair as Cousin Itt, but the voice was just the mumblings of a kid closely imitating the clay man, Mr. Bill, on "Saturday Night Live."

Here's the premise, in brief. Gomez takes off to Tombstone, Arizona, for a meeting, but has reservations about leaving Morticia in the care of his brother, Pancho. Three electronic wizards scheme to heist the family fortune on Halloween night while the Addamses are busily hosting a party for relatives. Morticia and Gomez look-alikes, along with a pair of hired musclemen, aid the thievery. Gomez returns, the crooks are scared off by the "natural" Addams surroundings, and the traditional Halloween festivities resume.

Although the movie was heavily hyped in the press, aired in a nice time slot, and garnered acceptable ratings, it earned concordantly crushing reviews. Earl Davis of the *Hollywood Reporter* slammed the movie, clearly defining its "tired plotline composed of gags that don't work, lines with no life and an overall deficiency of inspired lunacy that deals the show a deathblow from which it can never recover. Even the kiddie korps this is aimed at will find the final result insulting."

Producer David Levy said this of the endeavor: "The problem with all the efforts that were made to revive 'The Addams Family,' including this movie, was that the people who knew what 'The Addams Family' was all about did not have the right of final decision. Therefore, that show maybe reflected 40 percent of what it should have been. I was

*The Addams Family reunion movie that should have stayed buried (Courtesy of Goodtimes Home Video)*

not happy with it. But we suffered because we had the wrong director —nice chap, but he didn't know the show. We didn't have a writer from the show. [George] Tibbles was a friend of mine, but he didn't work on the show, therefore he was not indoctrinated—even [though] I tried to help, and Nat Perrin made some generous comments on the side."

Without extrapolation, he concluded: "That movie is a good example of network bureaucratic interference depriving audiences of the values that were inherent in the project."

Ted Cassidy, who felt typecast in Lurch-like roles and called the butler "an albatross" around his neck, admitted he has tried desperately to shake his "Addams" image ever since the mid-sixties. Yet in *Starlog* magazine he tells writer Joel Eisner that he enjoyed doing the reunion film:

Yeah, I did, because first of all, I got paid quite a lot of money for that. And second, I got a chance, for a week-and-a-half, to go over our histories with the others—Carolyn, John and Jack particularly and David Levy, the producer. We sat around like it was old home week . . . rehashed our lives . . . laughed and went out and got drunk a few times and that was terrific. I did [the movie] because I didn't want to let everybody else down. They all agreed to do the show. The fact that we were all able to reunite after twelve years is really astonishing. So I didn't want to be the rat who sank the ship by saying no.

"The show itself had too much happening, I felt," Cassidy said. "It was tough to follow—the big party with people rushing here and there. It could have been a simpler show."

## HALLOWEEN WITH THE NEW ADDAMS FAMILY

Network air: October 30, 1977, NBC
Color; videotape
Executive Producer: Charles Fries
Producer: David Levy
Writer: George Tibbles
Director: Dennis Steinmetz
90 minutes

### Cast

John Astin, Carolyn Jones, Jackie Coogan, Ted Cassidy, Henry Darrow, Patrick Campbell, Vito Scotti, Parley Baer, Felix Silla, Dean Sothern, Lisa Loring, Ken Weatherwax, Suzanne Krazna, Jennifer Surprenant, Kenneth Marquis, Elvia Allman, Jane Rose, David Johns, Clinton Beyerle, Terry Miller

# Animated Addams

Although Hanna-Barbera's "The Flintstones" parodied "The Addams Family" by introducing Weirdly and Creepella Gruesome, the jittery neighbors so clearly patterned after the Family, more creepiness from the famous cartoon factory was yet to arise. What began as a guest appearance on a two-part "Scooby-Doo" episode in 1972 flared into an animated series based on "The Addams Family."

Cartoon moguls William Hanna and Joseph Barbera naturally embodied the Addams Family around a spooky episode of "Scooby-Doo" (what other brand was there?), and casting the original TV stars for the vocal talent. Astin, Jones, Coogan and Cassidy provided the voices for their characters in these delightful episodes, which were drawn in the distinctive style of the original Charles Addams cartoons from *The New Yorker*. The animated Gomez appeared almost identical to Addams's squatty, balding, mustachioed Mexican type, rather than resembling Astin, the actor.

Producers enjoyed the positive reaction to the guest shot so much, they designed a new series around the characters and premiered a new, Saturday-morning "Addams Family" cartoon series in 1973 on NBC. Although it was popular enough to spawn a line of children's merchandise and successfully compete in the ratings race, it thrived only as long as its prime-time parent—just two seasons.

Press releases for the color cartoon explain: "Their gothic mansion has been replaced by a haunted trailer complete with piranha-filled moat —bats in the belfry—not to mention special pools for the family crocodile and Pugsley's pet octopus, named 'Ocho.' . . . With Lurch at the

156

The Hanna-Barbera cartoon series, which lasted two seasons, was closely patterned after the original Addams cartoons. (Courtesy of Hanna-Barbera Productions, Inc.)

*A rare animation cel from the Hanna-Barbera cartoon series (Courtesy of Hanna-Barbera Productions, Inc.)*

wheel they are off to visit the garden spots of America—Death Valley, the Great Dismal Swamp, and assorted ghost towns."

Coogan and Cassidy were the only originals from the sitcom to recreate their characters for the cartoon series; Astin and Jones were missed. But a budding young actress in one of her earliest jobs in entertainment supplied the voice for Pugsley Addams: Academy Award winner Jodie Foster, eight years old at the time. (Keep in mind that in the voice-over field, it is not unusual for a female to provide the voice for a male character. June Foray breathed life into Rocky the Squirrel, and Nancy Cartwright speaks for Bart Simpson.)

Veteran voice characterizationist Janet Waldo, who supplied the vocals of Morticia and Granny for this animated adventure, remembers little Jodie Foster and Jackie Coogan the most. "Coogan had trouble keeping his pages quiet, and had trouble with a lot of heavy breathing on the mike," she says. "He was a heavy smoker, and he wasn't accustomed to this type of work. Jodie had been around the block, as this type of work was concerned."

Waldo recalls Foster being accompanied to recording sessions by her mother, appearing "like a little lady, all grown up," she says. "Jodie spoke French fluently, and acted totally cool, no childishness at all. She was cute and honest. Very direct, and she came up with wonderful ideas. Look at her today, she's quite an actress."


### "THE ADDAMS FAMILY"

Network air: September 8, 1973–August 30, 1975, NBC
Executive Producers: William Hanna and Joseph Barbera
Producer: Iwao Takamoto
Director: Charles A. Nichols
Music: Hoyt Curtin
Music Supervision: Paul DeKorte
37 episodes (second season consisted entirely of repeats)


**Cast:**

Gomez . . . . . . . . . . . . . . . . . . . . . Lennie Weinrib
Morticia and Granny . . . . . . . . . . Janet Waldo

Uncle Fester .................Jackie Coogan
Lurch .......................Ted Cassidy
Pugsley .....................Jodie Foster
Wednesday ..................Cindy Henderson

With Josh Albee, Pat Harrington, Jr., Bob Holt, John Stephenson, Don Messick, Herb Vigran, Howard Caine (additional voices).

Uncle Fester: They're going to build a freeway!

Gomez: A freeway through our fair city?

Morticia: Well, a freeway may have its compensations. There's something rather musical about the sound of crunching metal.

# Voilà . . . a New Movie!

 Just when everybody thought the show was dead . . . when fans felt Fester had lit his last light bulb . . . as audiences assumed the Addamses had moved permanently into the morgue . . . the Addams Family is resurrected in a $30 million, star-studded feature film from Paramount Pictures. Fester rides again!

Hold on to your hats, folks—this is not a TV reunion film starring cadavers and ghosts, although the mere thought would probably please Grandaddy Chas. Nor is this a true replica of the television family audiences so identify with. Maybe it's a compromise between the readers of *The New Yorker* and of Addams's books, and those who affectionately revere the tube's version.

Clearly stated in the film's massive advance publicity campaign: the "screenplay was inspired by the mordant good humor of some 1,300 cartoons drawn by Charles Addams and largely published in *The New Yorker* magazine, *not* by the television series of the 1960s." Screenwriters Caroline Thompson (who penned *Edward Scissorhands*), Larry *(Beetlejuice)* Wilson, and Paul Rudnick may claim they were not scraping the television bowl, but obviously a fan of the cult hit had some involvement. Maybe the ghosts of Jackie Coogan, Carolyn Jones, and Ted Cassidy? And funny, but extensive prepromotion for the feature included teasers in theaters across the country that emphasized the TV theme song during previews.

Fans of Charles Addams and the Family—in any facet of their exposure—must consider this:

*New Thing: Magician Chris-
topher Hart supplies his
hand in the new film (Photograph by Stephen Cox)*

*Posing for a snapshot on the set, Christina Ricci and Jimmy Workman, who
portray Wednesday and Pugsley in the new feature film (Photograph by Stephen Cox)*

• The family from *The New Yorker* never had a name; therefore, the title *The Addams Family* derives from the TV show.

• None of Charles Addams's characters were ever named until the TV show. The same names are retained in the film.

• Elements such as Gomez's ever-present cigar, the sprinkle of French phrases that boil his passion, and his grabbing Morticia's arm and kissing it up to her neck were contributions by the TV cast, and re-created in the new film.

• The TV Addamses were a wealthy lot, and this thread appears again in the film. They could have appeared rich *or* poor based on the cartoons alone.

Many, many other basic, conscious, and not-so-obvious factors, so deeply rooted in the minds of TV fans, surface in this film, which is employing a special publicity campaign to stress its attempted "fresh approach." Won't this confuse audiences?

The dilemma was similar with *Batman;* many who plunked down the big bucks to see a first-rate film in a theater expected to be serenaded by Neal Hefti's popular TV theme, witness a sixty-year-old Adam West in blue tights, cowl, and cape, and see the Batmobile burst flaming from the BatCave. But none of this happened in the inspired, dark big-screen success starring Michael Keaton and Jack Nicholson.

As *New York Post*'s chief film critic Jami Bernard points out, "They're still creepy and kooky, mysterious and spooky, but *this* Addams Family lives in a different zip code. They're all back for the movie, same names, different actors."

Academy Award–winning actress Anjelica Huston, tall and thin, plays Morticia with the touch of class and elegance required to match the original Charles Addams cartoon matriarch closely. "I'm most prone to playing witches and ghouls and peculiar people," she says, alluding to her role in *The Witches.* Ironically, she recalls, a book of Charles Addams cartoons was permanently shelved in the bathroom of St. Clarens, the Irish estate where she grew up. Who could have known this might be inspiration for her later role?

Opposite her, as Gomez, is Raul Julia, the Puerto Rican actor who has starred on Broadway and in films such as *Kiss of the Spider Woman* and *One from the Heart.* Julia portrays Gomez with a zest similar to

Astin's, yet features natural bulging eyes à la Don Knotts's Barney Fife and like the original cartoon Addams patriarch.

The two-hour feature centers around Uncle Fester's reunion with the rest of the brood after a sustained absence in the Bermuda Triangle, a victim of amnesia. The role of Fester Addams (now identified as Gomez's brother) was awarded to character actor Christopher Lloyd, known to TV audiences as spacey Jim Ignatowski on "Taxi" and to movie fans as Dr. Emmet Brown in the *Back to the Future* epics. Lloyd might appear a bit thin for the puffy character we know and love, though we *have* seen him bald (in *Who Framed Roger Rabbit?*). Director Barry Sonnenfeld admitted to reservations. "We suspected he was too thin for the role," he told Jami Bernard. "We were thinking of more sort of round people. I talked to Danny DeVito, but he wasn't interested. We kept coming back to Chris, and finally shot tests with and without prosthetics. We tried rounder heads for him, but it looked like he had stepped off the set of *Dick Tracy*. So two days before shooting, we decided to shave his head and give him a fat suit."

This new film version, which the movie industry expects to be a mega-hit, was constructed with the Addams cartoons as guidelines. Producer Scott Rudin says he was probably destined to make this film: as a child, he built a model of the "Addams Family" house as offered in the sixties by Aurora. He told Bernard that the movie would be "less broad, more substantial than the TV series, less jokey. It's nice that the TV show gives us a built-in awareness for the audience we want, but if we simply meant to exploit the recognition of the title, we wouldn't have gotten the actors or the money."

The film's opening shot stems directly from one of Charles Addams's best cartoons: it's a bird's-eye view of the family crowded around a smoldering cauldron of hot oil. They are aloft in the cupola of the mansion, about to drench some festive Christmas carolers below. Another scene weathering a transition from off-the-wall cartoon to on-screen scream has Wednesday Addams chasing her brother with a sword. "You shouldn't use that on your brother," Morticia gently chides her, removing the sword and handing Wednesday an axe.

Expected to be the film's pièce de résistance is the "Mamushka" scene, where seventy-five waiflike extras in bizarre costumes fill the Addams ballroom. The ballroom scene may be reminiscent of the one

*The foreboding new Addams mansion, still under construction in February 1991. Notice the warning in the foreground. (Photograph by Stephen Cox)*

*Side view of the Addams mansion facade seen in the new film (Photograph by Stephen Cox)*

164   THE ADDAMS CHRONICLES

in *Chitty Chitty Bang Bang*. Raul Julia breaks into a sudden song à la the Marx Brothers' *Duck Soup*. "The movie literally stops in its tracks, as Raul dances, flips Chris Lloyd thirty feet in the air, [and] juggles knives," says director Sonnenfeld. "There's a point-of-view shot of a knife going down into Chris Lloyd's tonsils that will make studio executives cringe." Midget actress Patty Maloney, who plays Cousin Lois, performs cartwheels across the ballroom floor, while the crowd of crazy Addams relations and two-headed partiers dance the night away to music from the band. Be sure to notice the one-armed bass player: it's Eugene "Pineapple" Jackson, a short, bald black man who started in show business as one of the original "Our Gang" troupe.

Carel Struycken, the giant from TV's "Twin Peaks," plays Lurch. Pugsley and Wednesday are Jimmy Workman, in his film debut, and Christina Ricci, seen recently in *Mermaids* with Cher. Young Jimmy Workman, a dead ringer for the cartoon version of Pugsley, won the role accidentally when he accompanied his sister to an audition for the film. She was not selected, but producers spotted Jimmy and ultimately hired him, providing an acting debut. Five-foot John Franklin, who starred in Stephen King's filmed version of *Children of the Corn,* dons the mass of brown hair as Cousin Itt ("supported by a neck brace that helps hold the twenty-five-pound costume," he says) for a few brief scenes and says he'll provide Itt's voice as well.

Magicians and mimes were auditioned for the all-important role of Thing—after all, this could not be just *any* hand. Chosen was veteran magician Christopher Hart, who regrets that only his right hand will debut, but expects great "Things" to come from the film. "This project affords me the opportunity to create the ultimate form of magic," says Hart, twenty-nine, who has performed illusions professionally for nearly ten years. "My hand is flexible enough to project emotion. It has personality. Thing is likable, kind of childlike, and he's a practical joker." Fitted with a prosthesis of a stub wrist, Thing comes out of his box for the film and darts around as a disembodied hand gone wild. He runs up stairs alongside Gomez, plays chess with him, and, in a climactic scene, even races to save Morticia. The hero of the film? Wait and see for yourself. But Thing, via Hart, worked long hours on the set, just like Julia and Huston. The special-effects engineers, many of whom worked on the *Nightmare on Elm Street* films, optically—and timestakingly—

eliminated the rest of Hart's body from the footage. Some scenes involved a specially cast replica of Hart's hand, transformed into a mechanical limb operated by radio.

Hart, who once was employed as a gravedigger, was coincidentally nicknamed Lurch by his uncle years ago because of his six-foot-plus height. Hart's long and slender fingers as Thing may open up a can of worms with publicity involving *The Addams Family* but Hart would rather open a can of Coke—maybe a commercial campaign starring "the real Thing"?

Most of the cast will be hounded for interviews, although as a rule, Christopher Lloyd partakes with no press. In a rare interview during production, Raul Julia took a few moments from fencing lessons and line memorization to speak to me of *his* Gomez. Did he pattern it after John Astin's Latin lunatic?

"I didn't make a point of being different from the TV show or Astin," he says in a heavy Hispanic accent. "I saw parts of the show in passing, but I've never really watched a whole show. He did influence me a little bit. He had a kind of rascally essence that I use. John Astin gave me that inspiration, and I use that quality he had in the TV series."

Julia feels that *The Addams Family* may rank as one of his favorite projects, next to his critically acclaimed role in *Romero,* a film about the archbishop of San Salvador who was slain for his humanitarian work.

His film family is quite different from his own, says Julia, who is married and the father of two sons. "This is a weird family that enjoys pain and depression," he explains, laughing. "It says something at the same time. I think in a way we attempt to be so perfect that we don't allow stuff like anger, depression, and pain to come in, and we get so tense about it. We don't accept those things. The Addamses not only accept them, they welcome them, therefore they are happier."

Most of the indoor production was shot on the exact same soundstage that housed the television show twenty-five years ago: Hollywood Center Studios, formerly Francis Ford Coppola's Zoetrope Studios, and before that General Service Studios in the 1960s. The production occupied more than one stage, with the centerpiece Addams house on soundstage 3/8. (For outdoor shots, a larger-scale front facade of the house was built in the Burbank hills.) The main set includes Morticia's solarium of dead plants and prickly branches, Gomez's playroom and mess of wrecked trains, the grand entryway to the home, a library, and a small portrait gallery of wacky Addams ancestors. (Notice the portrait of Gomez as a baby holding a giant Havana cigar.) Dark and sinister like the original cartoons suggest, this lived-in home is perfectly decorated for big-screen audiences, who will enjoy its scope. But don't expect a mounted swordfish with a leg hanging out, or a two-headed tortoise centerpiece. This *Addams Family* is far from the television show in some aspects—*most* aspects, I suspect.

David Levy has one fear about the new film: that his television creation may be destroyed in the process. "I think it would be a great disappointment to the 'Addams Family' fans if they tamper with the basic nature of the characters as we created them," he says sternly. "When I say 'we,' I mean the whole team involved. That is the risk they take not involving any of those responsible for the TV series, which is basically me and Nat Perrin."

John Astin says, "Based on my relationship with the public, I know they're gonna expect me in the movie. I just hope they understand that I didn't refuse to do it. I would have loved to have done it. I love the character. It's an extension of my own personality."

What might the late Charles Addams think? Probably that, good or bad, if it tingles the spine and shivers the shoulders, 'tis good. In his thick Hispanic speech, Raul Julia stresses that the film is fun: "As Anjelica says, it's bin a rump!"

He means romp. But then . . . maybe he doesn't.

# Family Plots
## (in order of broadcast)

### "THE ADDAMS FAMILY"

Broadcast History:
    Network premiere: September 18, 1964
    Last prime-time telecast: September 9, 1966
    ABC-TV; Fridays, 8:30–9:00 P.M.
Based on characters created by Charles Addams
Developed for television by David Levy, executive producer
Producer: Nat Perrin
Associate Producer: Herbert W. Browar
Music: Vic Mizzy
Director of Photography: Arch R. Dalzell
Art Director: Edward Ilou
Set Decorator: Ruby Levitt
Production company: Filmways TV Productions, Inc.
Current syndicator: Orion Television Syndication

### Cast

Gomez Addams . . . . . . . . . . . . . . . John Astin
Morticia Frump Addams . . . . . . . . Carolyn Jones
Uncle Fester . . . . . . . . . . . . . . . . . Jackie Coogan
Lurch . . . . . . . . . . . . . . . . . . . . . . . Ted Cassidy

168

Grandmama Addams . . . . . . . . . . Blossom Rock
Wednesday Friday Addams . . . . . . Lisa Loring
Pugsley Addams . . . . . . . . . . . . . . Ken Weatherwax
Cousin Itt . . . . . . . . . . . . . . . . . . Felix Silla
                        (voice provided by Tony Magro)
Thing . . . . . . . . . . . . . . . . . . . . . . the hand of Ted Cassidy

GC: Guest cast
BD: Broadcast date (first run)

**First Season**

### 1. The Addams Family Goes to School

Teleplay: Ed James and Seaman Jacobs
Director: Arthur Hiller

Morticia decides to keep the children home from school because she is horrified by the fairy tales they are subjected to. Mr. Hilliard, a truant officer, pays an official visit to the Addams home to investigate. GC: Allyn Joslyn, Madge Blake, Rolfe Sedan, Nydia Westman. (Sidelights: This is the brief pilot script expanded as the premiere episode. The "train crash" scene was footage shot for the pilot presentation. This is the only episode using exterior footage of a real house.) BD: September 18, 1964.

### 2. Morticia and the Psychiatrist

Teleplay: Hannibal Coons and Harry Winkler
Director: Jean Yarbrough

When Pugsley abandons his pet octopus to befriend a puppy, wear a Boy Scout uniform, and play baseball, Gomez and Morticia fear their child is becoming normal. Distraught, they seek counsel from Dr. Black, a psychiatrist. GC: George Petrie. BD: September 25, 1964.

*John Astin and Allyn Joslyn, playing a truant officer, inspect Wednesday's headless doll. (Courtesy of Tod Machin)*

*Gomez fears poor Pugsley is deranged when he joins the Boy Scouts and plays with a puppy. (Courtesy of Milton Moore)*

### 3. Fester's Punctured Romance

Teleplay: Jameson Brewer
Director: Sidney Lanfield

Uncle Fester decides it's time for him to find a mate. Through a matrimonial column in the newspaper, he conducts a search and mistakes Miss Carver, a door-to-door cosmetics saleslady, for someone replying to his ad. GC: Merry Anders, Robert Nunn. BD: October 2, 1964.

### 4. Gomez, the Politician

Teleplay: Hannibal Coons and Harry Winkler
Director: Jerry Hopper

For the city council election, Gomez backs a candidate who vows to drain the town's unsightly and odoriferous bogs. Morticia feels the "lovely" bogs should remain, but Gomez assures her that all politicians do the opposite of their campaign promises. GC: Allyn Joslyn, Eddie Quillan, Bill Baldwin, Bob Le Mond (reporter's voice). BD: October 9, 1964.

### 5. The Addams Family Tree

Teleplay: Hannibal Coons, Harry Winkler, and Lou Huston
Director: Jerry Hopper

Gomez and Morticia trace their family genealogy after being accused by a snooty neighbor child that they lack proper breeding. GC: Frank Nelson, Jonathan Hole, Kim Tyler, Rolfe Sedan. BD: October 16, 1964.

### 6. Morticia Joins the Ladies League

Teleplay: Phil Leslie and Keith Fowler
Director: Jean Yarbrough

Gorgo the circus gorilla becomes one of the family, and Pugsley trains the beast to do house chores. Morticia invites the Ladies League to

*A Halloween publicity pose
(Courtesy of Howard Frank
Archives)*

*The Addamses and the Clampetts domesticated the same gorilla at the same
studio during the same season. The beast was played by George Barrows.
(Personality Photos, Inc.)*

tea and the gorilla shocks the guests. GC: George Barrows, Dorothy Neumann, Peter Leeds, Pearl Shear. BD: October 23, 1964.

## 7. *Halloween with the Addams Family*

Teleplay: Keith Fowler and Phil Leslie
Director: Sidney Lanfield

Two bank robbers hide out at the Addams house, mistaken for trick-or-treaters by Gomez and Morticia. The robbers abandon previous plans and remain at the Addams house attempting to rob the family. GC: Skip Homeier, Don Rickles, George Barrows. BD: October 30, 1964.

## 8. *Green-Eyed Gomez*

Teleplay: Phil Leslie and Keith Fowler
Director: Jerry Hopper

Gomez becomes jealous when a former suitor of Morticia arrives for a visit. Instead, the suitor—con man Lionel Barker—decides to channel his attention to Mildred, the new maid, when he learns she has invested successfully in the stock market. GC: Del Moore, Pattee Chapman, Jimmy Ames. BD: November 6, 1964.

## 9. *The New Neighbors Meet the Addams Family*

Teleplay: Hannibal Coons and Harry Winkler
Director: Jean Yarbrough

Honeymoon couple Hubert and Amanda Peterson lease the house next door to the Addams monstrosity, but their wedded bliss turns to terror as they meet the Addams Family in their natural—er, *un*natural—surroundings. GC: Peter Brooks, Cynthia Pepper, Eddie Marr. BD: November 13—Friday the thirteenth—1964.

### 10. Wednesday Leaves Home

Teleplay: Harry Winkler and Hannibal Coons
Director: Sidney Lanfield

Little Wednesday packs up her spider and runs away after being scolded for using Uncle Fester's dynamite instead of her own. Gomez and Morticia decide to let the Bureau of Missing Persons handle the search. GC: Jesse White, Ray Kellogg. BD: November 20, 1964.

### 11. The Addams Family Meet the V.I.P.'s

Teleplay: Keith Fowler and Phil Leslie
Director: Sidney Lanfield

Visiting dignitaries from an Iron Curtain country assume the Addamses are the typical uncultured American family. After witnessing Morticia's carnivorous plants and Uncle Fester's penchant for electricity, the officials conclude that Americans have vastly progressed in technology. GC: Stanley Adams, Vito Scotti, Frank Wilcox. BD: November 27, 1964.

### 12. Morticia, the Matchmaker

Teleplay: Hannibal Coons and Harry Winkler
Story: Maury Gerahty
Director: Jerry Hopper

Morticia and Gomez aid Cousin Melancholia snag a man she has her eyes on; her previous marital prospects have all joined the Foreign Legion. GC: Hazel Shermet, Lee Goodman, Barry Kelley, Hal Baylor, Lennie Bremen. BD: December 4, 1964.

## WEDNESDAY'S RUNAWAY NOTE

*(composed by Wednesday and Pugsley Addams)*

DEAR MOTHER AND FATHER,

I HATE YOU.

LOVE,

WEDNESDAY

P.S. DON'T BOTHER
LOOKING FOR ME
BECAUSE I'M NOT
ANYWHERE.
GOODBYE.

W.

### 13.  Lurch Learns to Dance

Teleplay: Jay Dratler, Jerry Seelen, and Charles Marion
Story: Jay Dratler
Director: Sidney Lanfield

Lurch confesses to be a wallflower at social events, so Gomez and Morticia convince him to take dance lessons for the upcoming Butlers' Ball. Morticia teaches him some gaucho steps; Gomez, tangos; and little Wednesday instructs ballet. GC: Jimmy Cross, Penny Parker. (Sidelight: The choreography is by Jack Baker.) BD: December 11, 1964.

### √ 14.  Art and the Addams Family

Teleplay: Harry Winkler and Hannibal Coons
Director: Sidney Lanfield

Gomez sends for unemployed artist Sam Picasso of Spain to teach Grandmama how to paint in the abstract. GC: Vito Scotti, Hugh Sanders. BD: December 18, 1964.

### 15.  The Addams Family Meets a Beatnik

Teleplay: Henry Sharp and Sloan Nibley
Story: Jack Raymond
Director: Sidney Lanfield

Swinging cool-cat Rockland Cartwright III crashes his motorcycle in front of the Addams house and takes refuge with the family. Like, man, he has trouble diggin' those cats, and the Addamses find "Rock" an oddity as well. Nevertheless, the family befriends him and throws a groovy birthday bash in his honor. GC: Tom Lowell, Barry Kelley, Barry Brooks. BD: January 1, 1965.

*Feisty Mother Lurch (Ellen Corby) pays a visit to her son. (Courtesy of Ellen Corby)*

*"Hurray for Captain Spaulding!" This candid photo captures Felix Silla without the bottom truss of Cousin Itt's hair. (Courtesy of Felix Silla)*

## 16. The Addams Family Meets the Undercover Man

Teleplay: Harry Winkler and Hannibal Coons
Director: Arthur Lubin

A government agent hires the mailman, Mr. Briggs, to invade the Addams household and investigate rumors that coded messages are being transmitted by someone in the family. GC: Norman Leavitt, Rolfe Sedan, George Neise. BD: January 8, 1965.

## 17. Mother Lurch Visits the Addams Family

Teleplay: Jameson Brewer
Director: Sidney Lanfield

Lurch attempts to conceal his employment as the Addams household butler from his tiny mother, who is visiting. Fester and Grandmama bail out when Gomez and Morticia want to pretend to act as Lurch's servants. GC: Ellen Corby. BD: January 15, 1965.

## 18. Uncle Fester's Illness

Teleplay: Bill Lutz
Director: Sidney Lanfield

Uncle Fester becomes an "outing pooper" as his electrical output fails just as the family is planning an outing. A doctor is summoned to cure him. GC: Lauren Gilbert, Loyal "Doc" Lucas. (Sidelight: Watch and listen closely. The camera zooms in for a close-up of Thing's box atop the harpsichord; without cutting, the shot widens and you can hear the dolly roll from under the harpsichord to hastily remove assistant director Jack Voglin from beneath it and just out of the camera's eye. Voglin was providing his hand for Thing because Ted Cassidy was playing the harpsichord.) BD: January 22, 1965.

## 19. The Addams Family Splurges

Teleplay: George Haight and Lou Huston
Story: George Haight
Director: Sidney Lanfield

The family consults Whizzo, a wacky computer contraption, to figure the possible cost of rocketing to the moon for a vacation. The estimate: slightly more than one billion dollars. GC: Roland Winters, Olan Soulé, Bill Baldwin (track announcer). BD: January 29, 1965.

## 20. Cousin Itt Visits the Addams Family

Teleplay: Henry Sharp
Story: Tony Wilson
Director: Sidney Lanfield

Gomez uses his influence with the park commissioner to get Cousin Itt a job at the local zoo. Commissioner Fiske assumes Itt belongs *behind* the cages. GC: Alan Reed, Bill Baldwin (radio announcer). BD: February 5, 1965.

## 21. The Addams Family in Court

Teleplay: Harry Winkler and Hannibal Coons
Director: Nat Perrin

Gomez becomes Grandmama's lawyer after she is arrested for setting up a fortune-telling booth in the Addams living room. GC: Hal Smith, James Flavin, Lela Bliss, Gail Bonney, Ray Walker. (Sidelight: In court, Gomez cites cases such as *"Voglin* vs. *Browar,"* borrowing names from some of the show's production personnel—Jack Voglin, Herb Browar, et al.) BD: February 12, 1965.

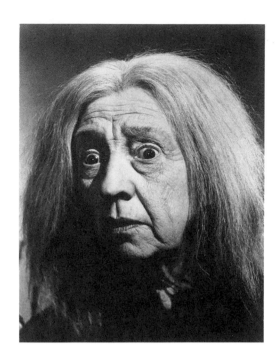

*Blossom Rock was Jeanette MacDonald's sister. (Personality Photos, Inc.)*

*Ted Cassidy released a single called "The Lurch" in 1965. (Personality Photos, Inc.)*

## 22. Amnesia in the Addams Family

Teleplay: Phil Leslie and Keith Fowler
Director: Sidney Lanfield

Gomez objects to the Addams homestead after he is hit in the head by his own Indian clubs and suffers from amnesia. The family take turns clubbing him on the head to restore his memory. BD: February 19, 1965. *( " Very well — (gulp) Dollboy.")*

## 23. Thing Is Missing

*" He's so handy for passing " and fanning soup.*

Teleplay: Bill Lutz
Story: Lorraine Edwards
Director: Sidney Lanfield

*Lurch presents Thing with an ocarina; music is heard. ("p/r:p/3 /œ/3 9.")*

Gomez hires a private investigator to assist in a search for Thing, who has disappeared. The entire family is under suspicion. GC: Tommy Farrell, Charles Wagenheim, Ray Kellogg. BD: March 5, 1965.

## 24. Crisis in the Addams Family

Teleplay: Sloan Nibley and Preston Wood
Story: Preston Wood
Director: Sidney Lanfield

Uncle Fester applies for a job as an insurance salesman with a company that's threatening to cancel the Addams policy, judging the family too dangerous to insure. GC: Eddie Quillan, Parley Baer, Bebe Kelly. BD: March 12, 1965.

## 25. Lurch and His Harpsichord

Teleplay: Harry Winkler and Hannibal Coons
Director: Sidney Lanfield

Lurch is inconsolable when Gomez donates the family harpsichord to a museum. To cheer him, the family attempts to interest him in other pursuits, like drums and needlepoint. Finally, Uncle Fester and Gomez decide to build Lurch a new harpsichord. GC: Byron Foulger, Lennie Bremen, Ray Galvin. BD: March 19, 1965.

## 26. Morticia, the Breadwinner

Teleplay: Phil Leslie

Director: Sidney Lanfield

*[handwritten: Uncle F: "For my escort service — if they like Frank Sinatra, I'll be Frank" Sinatra: "Love is wonderful / the second time around" "Uncle Fester, I think that's a mistake" — Yeah, I think I'd better get another song.]*

Morticia assumes Gomez is broke when the stock market crashes, so she assembles the family to devise ways of making money. Morticia wants to give dance and fencing lessons; Lurch and Uncle Fester decide to run an escort service; and the children will open a beverage *[handwritten: (blog)]* stand specializing in poison extract. Finally, Morticia sells off some properties while Gomez unknowingly repurchases them. GC: Milton Frome, Maxine Semon, John "Red" Fox, Ceil Cabot. BD: March 26, 1965.

*[handwritten: ("Dear Thing" is selling pencils, 5¢) M; "Phony name — Jones?" F: "What kind of a name is that?"]*

## 27. The Addams Family and the Spacemen

Teleplay: Harry Winkler and Hannibal Coons

Director: Sidney Lanfield

Investigators from the MSO (Mysterious Space Objects) mistake the Addams Family for aliens while the family is enjoying a moonlight picnic and snail hunt. GC: Vito Scotti, Tim Herbert, Jimmy Cross, Bob LeMond (announcer's voice). BD: April 2, 1965.

## 28. My Son, the Chimp

Teleplay: Henry Sharp

Story: Don Quinn

Director: Sidney Lanfield

While practicing magic, Uncle Fester believes he has accidentally turned Pugsley into an organ-grinder's chimp. Gomez and Morticia treat the monkey as if it were their child. GC: Robert Nunn (Boy's Voice). BD: April 9, 1965.

## 29. Morticia's Favorite Charity

Teleplay: Elroy Schwartz and Jameson Brewer
Story: Elroy Schwartz
Director: Sidney Lanfield

Morticia prods the family to donate objects of art from the Addams home to a charity auction. These treasured items include Wednesday's headless Mary, Queen of Scots doll, the old flogging table, and a shrunken head. Gomez donates Pugsley's beloved wolf's-head clock, but decides to bid at the charity auction to retrieve it. Thing's box is accidentally donated as well. GC: Parley Baer, Maida Severn, Donald Foster, John Lawrence. BD: April 16, 1965.

## 30. Progress and the Addams Family

Teleplay: Bill Freedman and Ben Gershman
Story: Cecil Beard and Clark Haas
Director: Sidney Lanfield

Gomez has ignored notices that their mansion is to be condemned for a projected freeway. When the Addamses hear a series of loud explosions not traceable to any family members, they discover that the trees around the house are being blasted. Gomez considers moving the entire house to another lot and creating a new set of swamps. The city commissioner decides to reroute the highway when he learns that the Addamses have decided to become his neighbor. GC: Parley Baer, Natalie Masters, John Hart, Dick Reeves. BD: April 23, 1965.

## 31. Uncle Fester's Toupee

Teleplay: Harry Winkler and Hannibal Coons
Director: Sidney Lanfield

Uncle Fester's pen pal, Madelyn Cavendish Beauregard Faversham Firestone from Paris, Illinois, is coming to visit, and he is thrown into

*Fester tries a new do. (Courtesy of Howard Frank Archives)*

*Out of costume, Jackie Coogan speaks on the studio telephone. (Courtesy of Sammy Keith)*

*Courtesy of Sammy Keith*

a panic because he has described himself as a handsome, romantic type. Gomez and Morticia convince Fester he needs a hairpiece. GC: Elizabeth Fraser, Frederic Downs. BD: April 30, 1965.

## 32. Cousin Itt and the Vocational Counselor

Teleplay: Hannibal Coons and Harry Winkler
Director: Sidney Lanfield

Morticia and Gomez decide that Cousin Itt would be a wonderful marriage counselor and pretend to be a couple with a failing marriage. GC: Richard Deacon. BD: May 7, 1965.

## 33. Lurch, the Teenage Idol

Teleplay: Phil Leslie
Story: Carol Henning, Mitch Persons, and Ed Ring
Director: Sidney Lanfield
" Mizzy Records "

Lurch records a song at the harpsichord which eventually attracts swarms of screaming teenage fans to the house. The rest of the family thinks it is an invasion. GC: Herkie Styles, Laurie Mitchell, Noanna Dix, Pam McMyler, Jacque Palmer, Patrick Moore. BD: May 14, 1965.

## 34. The Winning of Morticia Addams

Teleplay: Charles Marion and Jameson Brewer
Story: Charles Marion
Director: Sidney Lanfield

Family members scheme to start a battle between Gomez and Morticia because Uncle Fester has heard that happily married couples should fight. GC: Lee Bergere, Jan Arvan. BD: May 21, 1965.

## Second Season

### 35. *My Fair Cousin Itt*

Teleplay: Phil Leslie
Director: Sidney Lanfield

Gomez and Morticia prepare a drama as a birthday surprise for Wednesday. Cousin Itt stars in the production, takes elocution lessons for his role, and develops a Hollywood star syndrome. GC: Sig Ruman, Jimmy Cross, Douglas Evans. BD: September 17, 1965.

### 36. *Morticia's Romance (Part 1)*

Teleplay: Harry Winkler and Hannibal Coons
Director: Sidney Lanfield

On Morticia and Gomez's thirteenth wedding anniversary, Morticia tells the children a bedtime story of how she and Gomez met. GC: Margaret Hamilton. (Sidelight: Carolyn Jones plays three roles: Morticia, the twenty-two-year-old Morticia, and her sister, Ophelia.) BD: September 24, 1965.

### 37. *Morticia's Romance (Part 2)*

Teleplay: Harry Winkler and Hannibal Coons
Director: Sidney Lanfield

Wednesday and Pugsley refuse to go to sleep until they are told the rest of the story of their parents' romance, which includes a flashback. Morticia reveals that Gomez originally courted her sister, Ophelia. GC: Margaret Hamilton, Edward Schaaf. BD: October 1, 1965.

### 38. *Morticia Meets Royalty*

Teleplay: Leo Rifkin
Director: Sidney Lanfield

Gomez's aunt Princess Millicent von Schlepp arrives for a visit accompanied by Lady Fingers, her disembodied hand-maiden. Thing becomes entranced by the other hand. GC: Elvia Allman. BD: October 8, 1965.

### 39. Gomez, the People's Choice

*"The Press." – "I'm Brown, from the Sun."*

Teleplay: Henry Sharp
Story: Joseph Vogel and Marvin Kaplan
Director: Sidney Lanfield

Gomez becomes a candidate for mayor after witnessing the incompetence of the present officeholder, Mayor Henson. GC: Parley Baer, Eddie Quillan, Jack Barry, Lennie Breman, Bart "Buzz" Greene. BD: October 15, 1965. *Bagpipes*

### 40. Cousin Itt's Problem

Teleplay: Carol Henning, Ed Ring, and Mitch Persons
Director: Sidney Lanfield

The family thinks Cousin Itt is losing his hair, so Uncle Fester experiments with his chemistry set to produce a concoction that sprouts hair. GC: Meg Wyllie, Frankie Darro. BD: October 22, 1965.

### 41. Halloween—Addams Style

Teleplay: Hannibal Coons and Harry Winkler
Director: Sidney Lanfield

To prove to the children that witches *do* exist, Morticia and Gomez attempt to summon one through a séance. GC: Yvonne Peattie, Bob Jellison, Don McArt. BD: October 29, 1965.

### 42. Morticia, the Writer

Teleplay: Hannibal Coons and Harry Winkler
Director: Sidney Lanfield

*\* Aunt Singe, left Salem — "She may be cinders, but she's a lady!"*

*Margaret Hamilton, best known for her role as the Wicked Witch in the film classic* The Wizard of Oz, *played Morticia's mother, Hester Frump. As Frump, she closely resembled the menacing Miss Gulch of Oz. (The Mark Collins Hamilton Collection)*

*An Addams Halloween tradition is bobbing for apples— and lobsters. (Personality Photos, Inc.)*

Gomez feels neglected when Morticia spends most of her time writing children's books. GC: Peter Bonerz. BD: November 5, 1965.

*"You've given up writing?" / "for the time being" // "Write your next book in French!"*

### 43. Morticia, the Sculptress

Teleplay: Harry Winkler and Hannibal Coons
Director: Sidney Lanfield

Gomez brings in seedy art dealer Sam Picasso to purchase one of Morticia's statues after art critic Bosley Swain shuns Morticia's work. GC: Vito Scotti, Hugh Sanders. BD: November 12, 1965.

### 44. Gomez, the Reluctant Lover

Teleplay: Charles Marion and Leo Rifkin
Story: Charles Marion
Director: Sidney Lanfield

Pugsley becomes infatuated with his teacher, Miss Dunbar, and sends her one of Gomez's old love letters. Completely consumed by the letter, Miss Dunbar visits the Addams house in pursuit of Gomez. GC: Jill Andre, Tom Browne Henry. BD: November 19, 1965.

### 45. Feud in the Addams Family

Teleplay: Rick Richard and Jerry Gottler
Story: Rick Richard
Director: Sidney Lanfield

Prompted by Morticia's invitation, Mr. and Mrs. Henry Courtney visit the Addams house for tea, hoping to meet a member of the social set who turns out to be Gomez's cousin by marriage. GC: Fred Clark, Virginia Gregg, Kevin Tate. BD: November 26, 1965.

## 46. Gomez, the Cat Burglar

Teleplay: Phil Leslie
Director: Sidney Lanfield

Morticia and Uncle Fester discover hidden loot in the storeroom and find that Gomez is the neighborhood burglar-at-large. While sleepwalking, Gomez unknowingly robs homes. GC: Ken Mayer, Bill White. BD: December 3, 1965.


## 47. Portrait of Gomez

Teleplay: Leo Salkin, Bill Lutz, and Henry Sharp
Story: Leo Salkin and Bill Lutz
Director: Sidney Salkow

Cleopatra the plant eats Morticia's favorite photo of Gomez. When the original photographer is located, it is discovered that he now works for the Department of Motor Vehicles, and Gomez must get a driver's license to have his picture taken. GC: Tom D'Andrea, Ralph Montgomery. (Sidelight: Mexican midget-actor Roger Arroyo plays Cousin Itt in this episode.) BD: December 10, 1965.


## 48. Morticia's Dilemma

Teleplay: Jerry Gottler and John Bradford
Director: Sidney Miller

A longtime friend of Gomez's, Don Xavier Francisco de la Mancha Molines of Spain, visits the Addamses with his daughter, Consuela. Morticia is concerned when she learns that Consuela has been betrothed to Gomez since his childhood and has arrived to claim him. GC: Anthony Caruso, Carlos Rivas, Bella Bruck, Yardena. BD: December 17, 1965.

### 49. Christmas with the Addams Family

Teleplay: Hannibal Coons and Harry Winkler
Director: Sidney Lanfield

Uncle Fester is chosen to slide down the chimney dressed as Santa Claus to prove the existence of St. Nick to the children. Fester gets stuck in the chimney, so Gomez, Lurch, Cousin Itt, and even Morticia and Grandmama each don a red suit and appear to the children. GC: Gregg Martell. BD: December 24, 1965.

### ✓50. Uncle Fester, Tycoon

Teleplay: Sloan Nibley and Preston Wood
Director: Sidney Salkow

Fester is smitten with a bearded carnival lady and borrows stamp money to mail her a proposal for marriage. Morticia applies a beard and poses as the bearded lady's mother to convince Fester he will have to work to support a wife. GC: Roy Roberts, Harold Peary. BD: December 31, 1965.

### 51. Morticia and Gomez vs. Fester and Grandmama

Teleplay: Sloan Nibley and Preston Wood
Story: Lila Garrett and Bernie Kahn
Director: Sidney Salkow

Morticia decides to hire a governess to watch the children because she thinks Fester and Grandmama are spoiling them. Insulted, Fester divides the house in half. GC: Irene Tedrow, Loyal "Doc" Lucas. BD: January 7, 1966.

### 52. Fester Goes on a Diet

Teleplay: Hannibal Coons and Harry Winkler
Director: Sidney Lanfield

*"The Addams Family" measured up to big audiences in the ratings. In their first year, 1964—65, they placed number twenty-three. (Personality Photos, Inc.)*

*Howard Frank Archives*

Another of Fester's female pen pals is coming for a visit, and he consults television fitness guru Jack La Grann to plan an exercise agenda and diet. GC: Jack La Lanne, William Keene, Peggy Mondo, Rolfe Sedan. BD: January 14, 1966.


### 53. The Great Treasure Hunt

Teleplay: Hannibal Coons and Harry Winkler
Director: Sidney Lanfield

Morticia and Gomez find Great-Grandfather Pegleg's treasure map and summon Captain Grimby to charter a boat for a treasure hunt. GC: Nestor Paiva, Richard Reeves. (Roger Arroyo plays Cousin Itt in this episode.) BD: January 21, 1966.


### 54. Ophelia Finds Romance

Teleplay: Hannibal Coons and Harry Winkler
Director: Sidney Lanfield

Morticia's sister, Ophelia Frump, falls madly in love with Horatio Bartholomew. Meanwhile, Morticia attempts to rejuvenate Cousin Itt's past romance with Ophelia. GC: Robert Nichols. BD: January 28, 1966.


### 55. Pugsley's Allowance

Teleplay: Harry Winkler and Hannibal Coons
Director: Sidney Lanfield

Pugsley wishes to supplement his allowance and finds his own job. He decides to become a medical assistant to Dr. Bird during an operation. GC: Parley Baer, Jack Collins, Natalie Masters, Robert S. Carson, Tim Herbert. BD: February 4, 1966.

### 56. Happy Birthday, Grandma Frump

Teleplay: Elroy Schwartz
Director: Sidney Lanfield

Gomez and Morticia plan to send Grandma Frump on an all-expense-paid vacation to a beauty farm for her birthday. Grandma assumes they want to commit her to an old folks' home. GC: Margaret Hamilton, George Petrie. BD: February 11, 1966.

### 57. Morticia, the Decorator

Teleplay: Gene Thompson
Director: Sidney Salkow

To sell the neighboring Addamses an insurance policy, agent Joe Digby allows Morticia to redecorate his home. Morticia gives Mr. and Mrs. Digby a stuffed vulture as a present. GC: Eddie Quillan, Jeff Donnell. (Sidelight: Observe—the Digbys' living room was actually the set used for Wilbur and Carol Post's on "Mr. Ed," which was filmed at the same studio. "Ed" had been canceled by this time, so the scenery was no doubt available.) BD: February 18, 1966.

### 58. Ophelia Visits Morticia

Teleplay: Art Weingarten
Director: Sidney Lanfield

Ophelia taunts Uncle Fester into joining the Peace Corps. GC: George Cisar. BD: February 25, 1966.

### 59. Addams Cum Laude

Teleplay: Sloan Nibley and Bill Lutz
Director: Sidney Lanfield

Sam Hilliard, former truant officer, now runs the private school where Wednesday and Pugsley are enrolled. Hilliard breaks under the pressure of dealing with the Addams children, and Gomez buys the school. GC: Allyn Joslyn, Carol Byron, Pat Brown. BD: March 4, 1966.

## ✓60. Cat Addams   *Split + missing sone*

Teleplay: Paul Tuckahoe
Director: Stanley Z. Cherry

Dr. Marvin P. Gunderson is summoned to examine Kitty Kat, the family's ailing pet lion. Morticia realizes the doctor is the one who needs help. GC: Marty Ingels, Loyal "Doc" Lucas. BD: March 11, 1966.

## 61. Lurch's Little Helper   *Gaps in soundtrack*

Teleplay: Phil Leslie
Director: Sidney Lanfield

Gomez builds a robot to assist Lurch in the household work. Lurch allows the robot to do all the work and begins to feel he isn't needed. GC: "Robby the Robot." BD: March 18, 1966.

## ✓62. The Addams Policy

Teleplay: Harry Winkler and Hannibal Coons
Director: Sidney Lanfield

Uncle Fester accidentally incinerates the family's stuffed bear with his flame thrower, and Morticia files a claim with the insurance company. GC: Eddie Quillan, Parley Baer. BD: March 25, 1966.

## ✓63. Lurch's Grand Romance

Teleplay: Gene Thompson and Art Weingarten
Director: Sidney Lanfield

Lurch falls for one of Morticia's old school chums, Tiny Trivia. GC: Diane Jergens. BD: April 1, 1966.

### 64. Ophelia's Career

Teleplay: Harry Winkler and Hannibal Coons
Director: Sidney Lanfield

Morticia suggests to her sister, Ophelia, that she embark on a career. Ophelia chooses opera singing, coached by Cousin Itt. GC: Ralph Rose, Ben Wright. BD: April 8, 1966.

# THE ADDAMS HALLOWEEN POEM
## (A family favorite passed down through generations)

'Twas Halloween evening
And through the abode
Not a creature was stirring,
Not even a toad.

The jack-o'-lanterns are hung
On the gallows with care
To guide sister witch
As she flies through the air.

Drawn by eight beautiful bats
as she calls out to them:

Come, Flitter, come, Flutter,
come, Flapper and Flier.
Come, Chitter, come, Chatter,
come, vicious vampire!

## MORTICIA ON LITERATURE

Nauseated by the quality of current literature, Morticia set out to write her own novels—for children. Although she enjoyed the name of the Brothers Grimm, she detested their fairy tales. Killing off the nice dragons, witches, and ghouls—inhumane! What is this world coming to?

"Hansel and Gretel were juvenile delinquents for pushing a sweet old lady into a hot oven!" she remarked. "What was the name of that mean little girl who was so beastly to those three lovely bears?" she quizzed Lurch. "Ah, yes, Goldilocks! Trust a blonde to bring on trouble!"

Most sinister of all, Morticia thought, was Cinderella. "Can you imagine?" she said, choleric at the thought of her. "Those two good samaritans take her off the street and what does she do? The night they need her most, she runs off in a pumpkin!" This infuriated Morticia enough to right a wrong and scrawl her own version (with the help of her scribe, Thing), titled *Cinderella, the Teenage Delinquent.* The ending: "As the clock struck twelve, the police, summoned by the kindly stepmother, found Cinderella cowering in the ashes with the stolen glass slipper and yanked her off to the pokey."

A sure bestseller!

# Index

# About the Author

Stephen Cox, twenty-five, remembers flipping through pages of Charles Addams cartoon books at the local library when he was a youngster; this instilled a lasting fascination with the famed illustrator. Akin to Addams, Cox enjoys an occasional macabre twist to humor and shares an interest in unusual historical items (as a youngster visiting the Alamo, the author's favorite exhibit was an unforgettable wisp of Davy Crockett's hair preserved in a tiny glass locket). And like Gomez Addams, he enjoys a fine cigar. He presently resides in St. Louis, far from any cemeteries.

An ardent fan of TV's "The Addams Family" and "The Munsters," he now has written books on both. Other books by Cox include *The Beverly Hillbillies, The Munchkins Remember The Wizard of Oz and Beyond,* and (with John Lofflin) *The Official Abbott and Costello Scrapbook.*